FF&E

Furnish and Equip Your Vacation or Executive Property in Five Days

Anita Ericksen

FF&E: Furnish and Equip Your Vacation or
Executive Property in Five Days

by Anita Ericksen

Liaison Press
Vancouver, British Columbia, Canada

Published in Canada by Liaison Press, an imprint of
Creative Guy Publishing

ISBN-10: 1-894953-97-5
ISBN-13: 978-1-894953-97-9

FF&E

Furnish and Equip Your Vacation or Executive Property in Five Days

Anita Ericksen

Liaison Press
Vancouver | Canada

Thank you to my husband, Chris, whose unwavering confidence in my ability opened my eyes to what is possible. Great proof reading! You are a miracle. I love you.

To the kid whose smile lights up a room, my son, Brice. Your sense of humor, good nature and stubborn will (like your mother, God bless you) is evident in all you do. Good night, good night, I love you, I love you.

Thank you to Pete Allen who said this book was good (after he attacked and removed the abundance of semi-colons; I had splattered; throughout every page; that is). Thank you for making the book a reality.

Acknowledgements

To Anne-Brit Ericksen, for taking beautiful author pictures. I finally have some pictures of me (good in case I ever go missing).

To Jeff McFayden, for taking many of the photos in this book. Your love of the art comes through in your work.

Krista Luchka, for property set-up during the time the photos were taken. Thank you for coming over to proofread and share your thoughts. Oh, and it's Vivacity, not Viva City.

To Premiere Executive Suites, Edmonton (Bruce Wilde and Lana Tran), thank you for giving me my first job.

Forward

The cupboard door fell off its hinge. After seeing the sign on the front door that stated the last two exterminations were missed, after questioning the health of sitting on the sofa, this was the last straw.

Never mind the fact that there was not enough plates in the cupboard for the family or mold in the bathroom, for some reason it was the door unhinged; possibly because that was exactly what I was becoming.

"How do I make this a positive?" I thought. "Look for another rental," was my first thought. "No," I rationalized, "you create rentals; you know exactly what to do."

So, after a call to schedule a re-clean, and after tackling some of the issues myself, I got to work and called the owners. Stating what I do, they jumped at the chance for an evaluation. That was it; that was all they needed. The condo had "gotten away from them" and there was so much to do they didn't know where to start. I developed a plan for them and then spent the remainder of my vacation mulling over the possibility of summing up my work in an easy to follow format.

A little over one year later, a 5-day action plan was created.

Give people what they want before they ask or even realize they need it.

Contents

Preface...7

ChapterOne..11
Creating a Working Pallette

Chapter Two...23
Furniture/Media Shopping

Chapter Three...43
Inventory

Chapter Four..57
Furniture & Inventory Placement

Chapter Five...69
Art and Accessories

Chapter Six...107
Finishing Up

Chapter Seven...117
Going Above & Beyond

Chapter Eight..129
Final Words

Bonus Chapter..131
Guest Information Book

About the Author...137

Appendix A..140

Appendix B..142

Appendix C..144

Appendix D..146

Appendix E..148

Appendix F..154

Appendix G..156

Appendix H..158

Appendix I...160

Index..164

<u>Preface</u>

Congratulations! You have a vacation or executive property to rent. Whether you have purchased this book because you are a first time investor, a seasoned investor looking for a more streamlined approach to fully furnish and equip your next property or someone who needs to update their existing property, my wish is that this book helps you along your journey.

I can feel the nervous excitement you feel standing in your newly acquired property; you might actually be feeling a bit overwhelmed.

"Where do I start?" you ask yourself.

Without a guide, a few days of over-thinking on your part can easily turn into weeks. You might find yourself perusing a furniture store unable to make a decision or frequenting a kitchen and bath store too many times, because you didn't pick up everything the first, second, or third time. Naturally, you will revert to what you know, to your own style, but this isn't necessarily the best decision when it comes to fully furnishing and equipping for rent. Knowing where to spend your money, how to get the biggest bang for your buck, is where my expertise can help you. That white fabric sofa that you love may not be the best choice, and the pretty pattern china that you adore may not hold up during the normal (and not so normal) wear and tear of daily use. What is needed, and what this book illustrates, is how to simply, basically, and economically fully furnish and equip a property in as little as five days and create a property that will attract tenants, retain tenants, and ensure repeat tenants.

If you opt to use your time and energy to fully furnish and equip, and not go through an interior decorator whose specialty is vacation or executive rentals, then this book is for you. It will guide you on what to do and what to stay away from; giving you the knowledge to make well informed decisions.

If you wish to create a beautiful well appointed property, one that you can be proud of and one that does not attract only a select few, then this book is for you.

Together, we will create an incredible fully furnished and equipped property designed to increase your sales; retain and give you more repeat clients; as well as increase your bottom line.

A little background

In 2006, I purchased a condo in downtown Edmonton for investment purposes. My main objective was to rent it out. I did not want to take on the responsibility of managing it myself, so I contacted a property manager in the area who would manage my condo as an extended stay executive suite if I fully furnished and equipped it. I accepted this challenge and upon completion the owners of the leasing company were impressed with my efforts.

I look now at these photos and cringe at how elementary and unimpressive they are, but back then I thought I had created a masterpiece. Standing in the condo I had a "light bulb" moment – why not do this for those who don't have the time or are overwhelmed with the process? And thus began my career.

Since then I have fully furnished and equipped numerous properties loving each one more than the last one I did. I serve individual investors, property developers and leasing companies from Canada to Hawaii. I search for inventory with the forethought of:

Creating a lifestyle that is equal to or better than the tenant's current lifestyle.

This philosophy has served me well. My own fully furnished condo has been vacant only thirty days out of every year of ownership and with that in mind, I wish to show you how easily and affordably you can achieve this too.

Where it all began

I began writing this book as I sat in a fully furnished condo in Kihei, Maui that I so desperately wanted to re-decorate and re-equip. I was on vacation with my family and had not been hired to do this job, but it was taking every ounce of my self control not to 'help' the owners (well, I actually repositioned a chair, plant, and fan, but stopped myself there).

I write this book not only as someone who fully furnishes and equips for a living, but from the point of view of a tenant. I have been fully furnishing and equipping properties for executive and vacation rental since 2006. I have been renting vacation condos as a tenant since 2003.

I've stayed in a fair number of vacation properties throughout these years, some I will return to and some I will stay clear away from (unless, that is, the owners hire me). When it comes to renting your property as fully furnished and equipped it is not only location that attracts tenants, it is also presentation and in-house amenities. You are competing with not only other fully furnished and equipped properties down the road and next door to you; you are also competing with hotels.

My wish for you, as an owner of a vacation or executive rental, is to have repeat customers, to draw people to your property through the internet, to increase your nightly rate, to have tenants from other properties wish they had booked with you, and to have people recommend and refer your property to friends and family.

In fact, when it comes to sources of ideas for travel, 52% of people noted family and friends (*YPartnership/Harrison Group 2011 Portrait of American TravelersSM*); and 29% of travelers either always or often stay in the same rental year after year (*TripAdvisor Second Annual Vacation Rentals Survey, January*

2011).

We are going to use these statistics to our full advantage.

This book aims to take the guesswork out of refurbishing, furnishing, equipping and decorating. It aims to take what would be weeks of hard work and second guessing and shorten it to five days of confident purchasing and seamless organization. This book is an easy to follow guide, packed with information, designed specifically for the target market of individuals with average to above average income including vacationers; families; couples; singles; retirees and executives.

This book addresses refurbishing and then is divided into days, rooms and tasks with useful checklists to tear out and take with you on your five-day journey.

Good luck and have fun! The results will be worth it.

Chapter One

Creating a Working Palette – Prelude to Day One

Is your property in need of a refurbishing? Then this is where you start. Take a good look at your empty property from top to bottom. Walk slowly around, scanning the ceiling, taking notice of lights, looking down the walls, baseboards and down to the floor. Do this in every room, lingering on backsplash, countertops and cupboards. Notice everything from your baseboards to your ceilings. Inspect tile work, notice grout, check for nicks in walls and mildew and mold in the bathroom.

At the back of this book, you will find Appendix A. Appendix A guides you through your "walk about" with plenty of room to make notes. Mark down everything you see, so it is on hand and can be easily referred to; it is easy to forget something when there are a lot of projects on the go. Having a sheet to track the projects will be well worth it.

The imperfections you are searching for add up naturally over time due to day-to-day living. A few imperfections, i.e. a small dent in a wall; a pen mark on a cupboard door, are hardly noticeable. It is when the evidence of daily living accumulates that all of the imperfections become instantly noticeable, devaluing your property. Unless you have purchased a property that needs a major renovation, correcting these imperfections should be fairly simple. One only has to look on the internet to find do-it-yourself solutions to any household problem from fixing a leaking toilet to patching holes in walls.

Some sites I have found helpful are:

www.doityourself.com/scat/interiorimprovement
www.diynetwork.com/home-improvement
www.ehow.com/home-maintenance-and-repair

The nature of this type of work may induce you to hire a "jack of all trades," for the work involved encompasses a little bit of everything. Mark everything down on Appendix A and use your own judgment as to how you wish to proceed. If you decide to hire someone to fix the imperfections, having him/her refer to Appendix A will enable that person to work more seamlessly and more quickly than without having the guide.

Completing this first step in the process should not be overlooked. The end result will be a pristine palette to create a beautiful fully furnished and equipped home.

Wall colours

Imagine you are a tenant, how do the colours of the property make you feel in your core? Are you relaxed in warm tones or do you feel hyper amid vibrant colours? Your main goal is to create a relaxing environment for your tenant; a place to get away from work; a place to relax while on vacation; a place whose serene effect on the psyche transports through the photos that you will eventually post on your website. Colour alone will go a long way in achieving this.

The colour most appealing to tenants and the easiest colour to work with is an earth tone. By this I mean, a warm tone that is found naturally in our environment. We are aiming to bring in warmth with neutral colour. When working with a warm palette there are many varieties of colours I love. These neutrals are harmonious and uncomplicated resulting in a relaxing feel.

It is desirable to ask the paint experts at your local paint store if they give consultations, or know of someone who does, since lighting and undertones play a big part in this decision. You are dealing with not only paint colour, but how this colour can take on or clash with your existing lighting, cupboards, and flooring. The consultant should be able to come up with a variety of options that can be narrowed down very easily by discussing the desired outcome you wish to achieve.

Colour consultants are available at almost every paint store. If one is not available ask if they recommend someone or take a business card from their display. These are usually found near the cash register.

I have used many different types of paint and I must say that I do prefer Benjamin Moore™ paint. It holds up extremely well and the colours are absolutely amazing. To find a local retailer, open a browser and type the address:

www.benjaminmoore.com

and enter your city and province or state under "store locator."

Retailers will also have on hand colour palette brochures that you can take with you to help you decide on colour. Pick up a copy of "timeless neutrals". The lighter shades in this brochure should be your main base colour.

You can have a preview of this brochure here:

http://media.benjaminmoore.com/WebServices/prod/ ColorCards2012/timelessneutrals

Bear in mind your monitor calibration does have its limits and the actual colour may be a bit different than the colour shown.

Do not let this lack of vibrant colour scare you. We will be bringing in colour, but we are going to be doing that with art and accessories. It is ideal to have a clean and neutral colour as our backdrop.

Lighting

Is your property very dated? Was it designed and built many years ago with no refurbishing since? If the answers are "yes" to these questions then the lighting in the property will probably reflect this.

There is no reason to spend a lot of money for proper lighting. Appropriate pieces can be found at any local or major hardware store like Rona™, Home Depot™ or Lowes™. The lighting you choose should be simple. The lighting may not be opulent, but for our purposes it is perfect. Our main goal is to keep whatever you purchase from becoming dated over time and basic lighting is the best way to do this. Replacing outdated lighting will go a long way in making your property look modern and new.

Another way to modernize your property is to install pot lights that are about 3 to 4 inches in diameter. Don't go any larger for these will date themselves. Pot lights are one of the best ways to update a property. Installing them is not the easiest and most economical thing to do, but you may find that the trouble is worth the work and labour expense. Pot lights can be found inexpensively. If you decide to go this route, ensure the pots you buy have "easy to come by" bulbs. Some bulbs are so unique that they are only sold in the stores that sell the lights. Ensure the bulbs are mass produced and can be purchased at any commercial hardware store.

A nice look is to replace fluorescent lighting in the kitchen and bathroom with track lighting. Look for track lighting that has at least three bulbs though four or more is preferable. The more bulbs the track has, the more expensive the light will seem to be, even though this is not necessarily the case. It is all about perception.

A simple ceiling light, possibly with a fan, in the dining room, living room and bedrooms will go along way in updating your property as well as reducing heating and cooling costs by allowing improved air circulation. Spending a little bit more money here is worth it. Do not go for the least expensive set in this case, as these are mass produced and easily identifiable.

Kitchen/Bathroom

If your kitchen and bathroom are outdated, there are a few things you can do to that will make a huge difference without spending a lot of money and time.

If you find that through checking off items in Appendix A your kitchen and bathroom are in dire need of repair, by that I mean broken cupboards and chipped countertops, then a renovation is probably in order. If you find that the kitchen and bathroom just need some updating, then a few minor adjustments will make a big difference in the way your property is presented.

If you have enough money in your budget to do a complete kitchen and bathroom renovation, then by all means go for it. If you're working with a bit of a tighter budget replacing everything is just not feasible. The trick is to allocate the renovation funds you have available to create the biggest impact.

Begin with looking at your kitchen and bathroom with an objective eye and discern the biggest eye-sore in each room. Is it cabinetry, the countertops? Once that is narrowed down, this is the first project you will undertake. Continue on with the second biggest eye-sore, then the third, so on and so forth.

Updating by repairing and repainting is so much more inexpensive than replacing. Thanks to the internet, and people who post "how-to" videos, almost any project can be broken down into simple elements.

The sites **www.ehow.com** and **www.doityourself.com** are two sites that describe step-by-step instructions for renovating and refurbishing. **Doityourself.com** also has an added bonus of forums.

The idea here is get the biggest bang for your buck, in the least amount of time, so you can start renting the property as you intended to do when you purchased it.

Quick and inexpensive ways to update a kitchen/bathroom with a limited budget::

- Replace existing hardware with a modern updated variety.
- Replace existing faucets.
- Paint your cupboards or reface.
  - have a colour consultant and refacing company view your cupboards and make appropriate suggestions.
- Refinish your appliances if they are any colour except white, black or stainless steel; there are companies that will repaint your appliances making them look like new.
- If you want to try this on your own, hardware stores carry appliance paint.
- Use a tile and grout cleaner.

Flooring

We cannot speak of refurbishing without addressing flooring. For the purpose of vacation and executive rentals tile is best, for several reasons:
- Linoleum doesn't have good resale value and is prone to dents.
- Tile doesn't scratch like hardwood.
- Hardwood is also vulnerable to moisture and humidity.
- Tile doesn't hold dirt and bugs like carpet.

- Carpet is hard to clean and remove stains.
- Carpet may aggravate conditions such as asthma, and it may harbour mold and bacteria once wet.

I loathe staying in places with carpet, as I imagine what resides in the carpet and hate to walk around on it in my stocking or bare feet. I'm sure I am not the only one that feels this way. In fact, if you want tenants to take their shoes off upon entering your property you will have a much better chance of them doing this if there is no carpet in the property. Don't get me wrong, I love the feeling of warmth from a rug, but we will deal with this in a later chapter on area rugs.

Of the many types of tile you can purchase, I believe porcelain is the best bang for your buck though it is more expensive than ceramic. Porcelain has a colour consistency throughout the tile that ceramic does not have so it has a less damaged look if accidently chipped. Speaking only of expense, porcelain is much less expensive than natural stone in both product and labour cost. Porcelain, as well, holds a good resale value.

I recommend a tile colour of a medium to dark tan and a grout colour of the same, making it monochromatic. Tan or beige tiles and grout will keep looking clean longer. It will hide dirt and sand and will not show stains as easily as some lighter tiles and grouts. Ensure you put on a grout sealer. The sealer should be reapplied every year.

Window Treatments

Did your property come with curtains and/or blinds already installed or is this something you have to add or replace? The following guidelines will help you with your decision in this matter whether you are choosing window treatments, or critiquing what you already own.

Personally, I like the look of blinds. I believe they are easier to keep clean since you don't have to remove them to dust and wash them as you would with curtains. Liquid and food marks can be easily removed, making them resistant to stains.

If you prefer drapes, please remember that cleaning the drapes, as with dusting blinds, will have to be on your list of regular cleaning chores for your cleaners. Shaking out drapes or washing them to try to release stains may take longer than dusting and wiping down blinds. If you love curtains enough that you are willing to pay a bit more for curtain maintenance then by all means go with that.

The best colour for either blinds or drapes is neutral. By that I mean, a lighter colour that is tan or beige. These colours will keep your property looking modern for a longer period of time for these colours are not "faddish." These colours go well with any décor. They are safe and you can't go wrong.

If you are opting to go with a wooden blind, choose faux wood or a plastic matching your trim (if white) or coordinating with your flooring. Real wood blinds are an expense that is not justified. You want clean, not expensive. Faux wood blinds are made so well now that they are esthetically pleasing.

If your property does not come with black out shades or drapes I highly recommend installing these in the bedrooms. If you intend on having guests sleep in the living room it may be a good idea to install black out shades in this room as well. Vacationers think very highly of these; if you are installing them it is a great idea to mention that you have them on your website.

Hopefully you already have blinds and/or curtains in your property. If they match the criteria above then congratulations! You have just saved yourself some money. If not, then remove and replace. Nothing will date your property faster than drapes or blinds that do not adhere to the above mentioned guidelines.

If you are choosing to install these items yourself then now is the time to measure your windows. Appendix B, at the back of this book, is available to you to mark your measurements and tear out to take with you on Day 3.

Cleaning

Once the refurbishing has been completed, it is best to have your property cleaned inside and out before furniture and inventory arrive. Also, make sure all of your utilities are connected unless you want to be crying in your gin bottle that night. I have worked in a condo without utilities, in the dead of winter, and my time doubled with no water and tripled when the sun went down. Completing my project with a flashlight seems much funnier now than it did at that time.

Working from a clean slate will save you valuable time later on. Unless you are a contortionist, it is so much easier to clean an empty property than bend and stretch around your newly purchased furnishings and fixtures.

If you are cleaning yourself or decide to hire a cleaning company ensure they come the day before furniture purchase – Day 1.

Speak with potential cleaners about their range of cleaning and get references. You may also wish to get references from other owners of vacation or executive rentals. On this day, it is essential that the cleaners, in addition to regular cleaning, also:

- Wipe the inside of cupboards and drawers.
- Clean lights.
- Clean all appliances inside and out.
- Clean behind and underneath all appliances.
- Clean all shelving.
- Spot wash the walls including light switches and baseboards if, perhaps, you did not need to repaint.
- Wash windows.

- Clean the patio or deck.

Final Words

There are certain things that should be consistent throughout all vacation and executive properties:

- the feeling of relaxation,
- the look of cleanliness, and
- continuity.

There is nothing like a well put together property, a property where each room flows into the next. If one pays attention, they will feel a definite discord in a poorly decorated home and harmony in a well decorated property. For some, it is difficult to pinpoint why exactly the discord is occurring, only that it is ever present. A well appointed room goes a long way in making someone feel as if they are "home"— that relaxed, easy going feeling that is as warm and comforting as apple pie. Creating this feeling in your tenants is not difficult to achieve, and with consideration to different aspects, easily attainable.

Once all of the imperfections have been removed from your property, the next step is the purchase all items needed to furnish and equip your property. The next few chapters list projects and their timelines. This will help you with the organization of your project so your time is used effectively and efficiently.

First though, what is the cost to fully furnish and equip? Unless you are in the luxury market the average cost to fully furnish and equip will be approximately $11,000 (based on a one bedroom, two bath property of approximately 1000 sq ft):

Furniture
$7500[1]

---

1   *Add $2000 for each additional bedroom*

Art/Accessories
   $700
Inventory (Kitchen, Bathroom, Media, Miscellaneous)
   $2500
Deliver and Assembly
   $500

Of course, you can always spend more money depending on how high end you wish to go, but by following my recommendations you will create a lovely property that is priced in the mid range and looks higher end; a property where tenants will say, "Well, knock me down and call me Susan, this is nice!" You will create a property you can be proud of and your tenants will love staying in within five days. So, let's begin by getting acquainted with our time line.

Below you will find a graph illustrating a breakdown of the next five days. On Day One, ensure you make all calls necessary to organize this project to ensure your property is completed in a timely manner. Some items may not be relevant to your situation so just pick and choose what pertains to you.

Adhering to the below mentioned timeline is perhaps the most important thing you can do to make this entire process run smoothly. The effort involved to organize will save you hours and possibly days. I highly recommend it.

Day 1 / Date:		
Schedule services: • Book elevator for Day 3 • Book delivery drivers/ assemblers for Day 3 • Book house cleaners/ Maintenance Person and Concierge Service for Day 5 • Book property manager for Day 5	Furniture shopping: 6 hours	Quick clean up
Day 2 / Date:		
Inventory Shopping: 6 hours		
Day 3 / Date:		
Delivery drivers: AM Furniture Assemblers: PM	Placing inventory	Quick clean up
Day 4 / Date:		
Art and Accessory Shopping: 6 hours	Placing art and accessories	Quick clean up
Day 5 / Date:		
Final touches	Housecleaners/ Maintenance Person/ Concierge Service – late AM	Property Manager – early pm

Chapter Two

Day 1 – Furniture Shopping

Today is the start of your five day project with me by your side, guiding you. The next few days should run smoothly as you will be filled with confidence on what, how and when to purchase your inventory creating an amazing property that you will not only be proud of, but that will attract, retain and ensure repeat tenants.

After you have booked the outside services that will assist you in preparing your property for tenants it is time to go furniture shopping. Schedule a six-hour time block to choose these items.

When shopping for furniture, choose a company that carries mid- to higher-end furniture. As well, choose a store that has a warehouse with stock on hand. You're going to want to choose furniture that is only in stock. Ensure they will deliver within two days. Also, *and this is important*, ask how they handle damaged items. If the process seems arduous, choose another store. If they will replace a damaged item that same day, go with them. More than likely your furniture will be undamaged, but it is wise to check their policy to ensure no disappointment later on.

Only choose one store to complete your shopping if possible so you have leverage when asking for a discount. Ask about stain remover and purchase insurance.

Check if the delivery drivers can assemble the furniture that is purchased. The extra cost of this service is well worth the trouble of trying to do it yourself. If they do not, they more than likely have a list of assemblers they use and can refer. Call this assembler immediately to coincide delivery time with his or her arrival.

One more thing to ask is if the delivery drivers take away the boxes, plastic wrap, tape and general debris. Again, there may be an extra charge for this, but it is more convenient than hauling all your boxes to a recycling bin around corners, downstairs and into elevators.

With the furniture, we are creating a lifestyle that is equal to or better than your tenants' current lifestyle. In my line of work, I have seen many fully furnished properties that do not measure up. Of these, I am often hired to make them more attractive to tenants. Once tenants have viewed a property that has some forethought, they will more than likely walk away from a property that does not meet their expectations. Your property is going to be a front runner, a winner. We are staying clear away from creating those properties that tenants take because nothing else is available. These are not the type of tenants you want.

You want tenants that respect your property because you respect your property and you want tenants that love your property as much as you love your property. You want to know that the tenant inquired about your property because they were attracted to it rather than because nothing else is available. You want someone to be as excited to stay in your property as they are about the rest of their vacation.

It is so easy to pick out a property that was slapped together rather than one put together with some forethought. There is a huge difference between putting inventory in a property and creating a home with your inventory. We are doing the latter, and it will be well worth it.

At the back of this book you will find Appendix C which illustrates the furniture required for each room. There is no need to write down everything that is listed below on a separate piece of paper.

Our job is to find good solid pieces that will stand the test of time; pieces that are not only sturdy, but will still look good after years of use. Since I have been fully furnishing and equipping I have only once had to replace one sofa that was damaged. All of the furniture I have chosen is holding up nicely after 7 years. We will be choosing solid pieces and, as well, pieces that will not date themselves. We wish to have furniture that will still be stylistically current years after it was purchased.

I recommend that you purchase more streamlined furniture: furniture that has more straight lines rather than curved lines. Straight-lined furniture has been around for years and years and this furniture still looks just as good today as it did back in the 50s. Purchase comfortable seating that isn't fluffy or hard; chairs that are sturdy and beds that are comfortable. Stay away from anything too ornate, avoid carved wood; be trendy without being "faddish."

Ensure the furniture you choose for one room has the same colour of wood throughout. It is acceptable to choose different woods for different rooms, but if you decide to do this, to keep a flow going throughout the entire property, look for woods that are not that far apart from each other in tone. There is an exception to this that I will get to later on in the book, but for now, this is basic, and basic works in creating continuity. I have not seen your property and I can't get a feel for it, but there are elements of furnishing for rental purposes that should be very consistent throughout, and this is what I am stressing. When choosing wood colours, choose a wood that is in the medium to dark brown or black range. Stay away from light coloured woods, for these colours date themselves very quickly. Avoid expensive woods like teak strictly for budgetary reasons. A dark stained oak is less expensive and the effect will be the same. These colours have a classic yet contemporary feel. We wish to create harmony and continuity and having similar wood colours throughout your rooms is essential for this.

When choosing furniture, stay with a general style. Do not get specific with the area your property is located i.e. rattan in Hawaii or trees and animals carved in wood in Whistler. I say this for a few reasons: one, this type of furniture is so specific to a certain market that it is often priced higher than its counterparts; two, rattan in a bedroom is great place for breeding bedbugs to hide; three, carved wood has a maintenance issue all its own when removing dust and polishing. Don't get me wrong, we are definitely going to celebrate where your property is located, we are just going to do that through art and accessories.

Before we leave on our shopping expedition, please see Appendix D. Here, you can find a tear out sheet to record room measurements. I can't stress enough the importance of accurate room measurements. These measurements will ensure you do not purchase furniture too small or large for your room and you won't have to resort to your own hand and feet measurements.

> *Ensure you take your tape measure with you to the furniture store*

Bedroom

If the bedroom is a large enough size I would choose a king size bed over a queen size bed. King size beds are very attractive to tenants, often being a major reason for a tenant choosing to stay in your property. They are luxurious, and are often rare in fully furnished properties. Having one is worth mentioning on your website. Your main goal is to fit a king size bed, two night stands and, hopefully, one dresser or chest without the bedroom being cramped. Ensure you can walk around both sides of the bed. In other words, do not push one side of the bed up against a wall.

Always make sure you have two nightstands. If the bedroom is too small, readjust your choice to find a suite that has smaller nightstands. If the bedroom is still too small, purchase a queen bed and two nightstands over purchasing the king bed and only supplying one nightstand.

If the bed and nightstands fit nicely, but there is no room for a dresser or chest (by this I mean less than 24 inches from the dresser to the bed), you have two options:

One, insert a closet organizer with shelving or drawers for folded clothes as well as still making room for hanging clothes or,

Two, if you have a double door closet, check to see if the matching chest will fit in one side of the closet. Ensure you are able to open the drawers of the chest without opening both doors. One side of the closet will be for folded items and the other side of the closet will be for hanging items.

To make the room seem larger than it is, purchase a bed without a footboard. A footboard takes up another 6 inches or so and this could mean the difference between a dresser being placed on the opposite wall or not. Again, ensure there is at least a walking space of 24" from the end of the bed to the dresser. If there is less, a dresser or chest will not fit in this area comfortably. If this is the case, then you must consider how you will place your TV (which will be at least 32 inches) for this room. If you are mounting a television then all is good. If you are opting to place your TV on a stand then you must find a stand that is narrow enough to fit this space and comfortably hold a TV. I have found when I am ever in this predicament that a book/shelving unit works very well. A book/shelving unit is less wide than a media center, approximately half the width, but holds a TV safely and with ease. As for colour, since we are going with a piece that does not match the bedroom suite, I would not try to match the wood, in fact, I would do just the opposite and take a different colour all together being a darker colour than what you have. Do not purchase a lighter wood colour as this will look poorly decorated.

As well, platform beds seem to make a room look more spacious as they are not as high as a mattress with a boxspring, they look more upscale and you will be saving money as you will only have to purchase a mattress and not a box spring. If purchasing a platform bed, it is imperative that you check the slats to see if they are strong and solid. If the slats seem weak, but you still desire the bed, consider placing a piece of plywood where the slats are or cut your own 1x4s or 1x6s, creating a much stronger support for your mattress.

You will want to purchase a solid wood bed rather than one that is mostly made of particleboard. You may be tempted because of the price difference between these two, but it is not worth the hassle of the bed cracking under the weight of one or two people. You will be able to notice right away if the bed is flimsy and lightweight or not.

Mattress

Nothing is as important as a comfortable mattress to keep your clients coming back. Purchase a medium firm mattress, as this appeals to the majority of people, and ensure it is protected with a mattress pad or mattress encasements.

Mattress encasements resist bedbugs and stains. Insects are repelled and liquids do not soak into the mattress, but stay on top of the pad to be easily wiped off. The price point is no more expensive than a regular mattress pad without these additional resistant natures and well worth it. No one likes to talk about bed bugs, but it is something you must consider. One bad review could stop future bookings and start a cancellation frenzy, paralyzing your finances. These can be removed and washed on a regular basis. Mattress pads and encasements can be found at many linen stores including:

www.beddingtons.com
www.mattresscoverscanada.com
www.bedbathandbeyond.com

When purchasing a mattress ask if they offer a Stain Terminator fabric protector. This is the Nano Stain Terminator™ by Culp Home Fashions™. The protector forms a shield on the mattress ensuring stains and spills are repelled and do not soak into the mattress but bead and roll off. In addition to the stain protector, you may wish to incorporate the Antimicrobial Protection™ by the same company which protects against mold, mildew and microorganisms.

Dining/Dinette Area

I realize I am not there to see your space, but I also am aware of the "safest" type of table to purchase, and that is a circular table. A circular table takes up less space, has a nice curve in relation to your streamlined furniture and there are no sharp edges. To ensure the table you choose is large enough, consider the amount of people you allow in your property and multiply that amount by 24 (these are the inches one person would need on average), divide this amount by 3.14. The resulting number equals the diameter your tenants would need in order to feel comfortable. For example, 4 people multiplied by 24 and divided by 3.14 equals a 31 inch diameter.

Most properties will have a designated dining area; be it a separate room or a space shared with the living room. Most of the time you can distinguish this space by finding the dining room ceiling light. *Most of the time.* Positioning the table directly under the dining room light is the most obvious thing to do.

Sometimes, though, the light is not positioned properly making the dining room table obstruct an obvious walkway. It is always wise to remember that creating space is one of the most important elements to consider. The more space you have to walk, the less crowded and small the area will seem, even if you have the same amount of furniture. It is purely a trick of the eye.

If the dining table is obstructing a walkway, if you have to walk around it to get to another area of the property, there are a few things you can do. Sometimes all you need to do is move your table a few inches, 4 or so, to create the space you desire. Doing so will be hardly noticeable to your tenants, but will make all the difference in the world. If your dining light hangs down, investigate as to how much leeway you have with the cord. Often times, the cord is longer than what is showing and there may be enough length to drape that cord to a better location.

One other option that is a nice alternative is to install track lighting. Install a track light with four or five bulbs and positioning your table will be a breeze.

The dining room may be large enough to hold a credenza and this is a solid option though not mandatory. If you wish to purchase the matching credenza to your dining table, ensure there is at least 24 inches of room from the credenza to the closest dining chair. The dining chair must be positioned as if someone where at the table eating to get this measurement.

The chairs you purchase must be of good quality; iron is the strongest chair you can purchase, but I find wood will work well if the chair is made well. Again, heaviness is important, solid wood or iron is your best option. A broken chair is not something you will want to deal with as part of the regular maintenance on your property. As for the chair covering, a perfect type to consider is leather, either dark brown or black. Leather is so forgiving, especially around a dining table. It is easily wiped of spills and food and keeps looking good for years to come.

When it comes to saving money, purchase a less expensive table and sturdier chairs. There is no need to purchase a set that already goes together at your local store. A less expensive table flanked with leather parson chairs makes your entire set look high end and no one is the wiser. Match the wood of the table with the wood of the legs of the chairs.

As for bar stools, the dining table will more than likely be placed beside these items if you have a property with one large room encompassing the kitchen, dining room and living room. Ensure there is space to walk around between the bar stools and the dining room chairs and table. If it seems cramped, purchase barstools that have no back support. Look for stools that can be placed directly under the bar; like saddle stools. Stools with back support will take up another 6 to 8 inches of space that may hamper your tenants' ability to move around and be comfortable. Like the dining chairs, ensure these are sturdy.

Living Room

As with all the rooms, it is essential that the living room show its best while being very functional. The key here is to utilize this space to fit as much seating as possible without being overcrowded. There are many multi-functional pieces of furniture that we will discuss shortly.

Our dream would be to fit these essential pieces:

- sofa or sectional,
- loveseat or chair(s)/chaise,
- entertainment center,
- coffee and end tables

Of course, we know this all depends on the size. With my help, you will discover what is absolutely essential and what you can get away with not placing.

The living room I would say is one of the most difficult to write about, because unlike the other rooms, the living room can have extreme variability. Many elements need to be considered, such as light, irregular walls, where windows/doors are, and general shape. Of the many properties I have fully furnished and equipped, the living room is by far the area where the most creativity can come into play. There have been times when I have viewed a property only to look at the dimensions of the living room and wait for inspiration to come to me. It looks very much like I'm staring out into space with a blank mind, but the gears are turning. Other times, I have to sit with it and let my brain work it out while I carry on with other tasks.

First things first, let's start with one of the most important pieces in the living room:

Sofa

My first piece of advice is to get leather. I know I have mentioned the resilience of leather previously, but that is because I believe in it so much. Leather is so forgiving, it is cool in the summer and warm in the winter, it repels stains and odors. It adds the extra element of being upscale and looks rich. It is by far the best that you can get. When choosing your leather sofa, feel the leather; pinch it to ensure that it is thick and resilient. Talk to the sales person and tell him or her the purpose of your purchase. Of course, we all know that top grain Italian leather is amazing, but we can get away with leather that is not of this quality and still durable. There is also bonded leather. This is an option I have used in properties before and over the years the furniture has held up amazingly well. Bonded leather is leather that is made by applying adhesive to fibers of leather. The total leather amount is about 15%.

To be aware of your different options, the different types of leather are:

- Full grain/top grain – Full grain leather is leather in its most natural state. It is the most expensive and the softest type of leather.
- Split Leather – Less soft and less expensive than the full grain leather, it is more fragile therefore possibly more easily damaged.
- Nubuck/Buffed/Suede Leather – The surface of this leather is buffed to create a soft layer making it susceptible to stains from liquids, including water. Suede is not a good option for fully furnished suites.
- Bicast or Coated Leather – Polyurethane is added to the leather making it fairly durable. It is economical and often used in commercial establishments so you know it is resilient.

As for colour, I would choose a darker shade, either brown or black. I have used light coloured leather in rentals before, but it is because I have considered all elements. The properties I have used lighter leather in are rented for well over $6000 per month with no children or pets allowed.

A three-seat sofa or sectional is your best option. Even if you have to forgo extra seating because this is all you can fit in the room I would take this option over having a love seat and an additional chair. More than likely you will either be renting an executive property where the executive wishes to stretch out or have a family renting your vacation home. A three-seater or sectional caters to both types of tenants.

The cushioning in your sofa is very important. Speak to the sales person to ensure the foam inside the cushions is dense and long lasting. After a year of use, you do not want to have sagging cushions.

If you absolutely abhor leather and refuse to consider purchasing a leather sofa please ensure the sofa you purchase has removable cushion covers. The best advice I can give would be to take these covers to your local dry cleaner for stain removal and cleaning. This I would do on a quarterly schedule. You may be tempted to save some money by washing and ironing the covers yourself, but bear in mind that you take a risk on the covers shrinking and fading. Also, it is probably wise to schedule a quarterly upholstery steam clean to the back, arms and sides of the sofa.

Chairs/Chaise

If your property can comfortably fit a chair that is about 18-24 inches away from other furniture, you have two options. Purchase a matching chair or one that is a decorative piece yet still comfortable. If you like the idea of placing a decorative or designer chair purchase one in a colour that is not similar to your sofa colour. We are creating a focal point with the decorative chair and we do not want it to blend into the existing furniture. Ensure there is comfortable walking room to and from the chair. Trying to squish pieces together will look horrible. A chaise is an option that is beautiful and looks very upscale if you have at least a 24-36 inch space walking to and from it. Again, it can be part of the set of your existing sofa or be completely different.

Place the chaise or the chair(s) opposite or to the side of the sofa to create a conversation area. Placing the sofa opposite the TV is fine, but creating an area for conversation is also something important to consider.

Additional Sleeping

This book would be incomplete if I did not mention some of the different varieties of "hide away" beds available on the market. Even though the above aforementioned budget will be blown if you decide to take this route, the cost may very well be offset by the interest in your property from larger families.

> *Cost savings: Consider purchasing or making (if you're handy) the bottom part of a trundle bed to slide under other beds. Great for young children who wish to sleep in the same room with their parents.*
>
> *"trundle bed" + "your city"*
>
> *www.ehow.com/how_6692342_make-trundle-bed-frame.html*
>
> *www.ehow.com/how_2385932_build-trundle-beds.html*

Sofa Bed

One of the original versatile pieces, this type of sofa can serve as a seating area and an extra bed. Gone are the days of your typical "sofa bed" and hurrah to the days of ingenuity.

If you believe you need a sofa bed: if you want to advertise your property as able to have the most people sleeping there as possible, a sofa bed is an excellent option. They have come a long way and many are comfortable and look great.

Having a comfortable mattress is of the utmost importance. I have heard of individuals who have removed a thin mattress from a sofa bed and replaced it with a deflated air mattress to be inflated by the tenants should the need arise. I have also heard of removing an uncomfortable mattress and replacing it with a dense cushioned foam or a futon. These are pretty ingenious ideas and are definitely better than a thin uncomfortable mattress though most sofa beds now have mattresses that are more comfortable than previous years.

Your typical pull out bed, one where you would be removing top cushions then yanking up and out is really a thing of the past. Many companies make sofa beds that are converted by a release latch to bring the back rest down creating a queen. I love this idea. It is easy, the sofa cushions are then used either to sit on or lie on.

There are also sofa beds that release from the bottom for you to pull out, again without removing cushions and they prop up like an ironing board; again, brilliant idea.

Type "sofa beds" into your search engine (click on images) and you will see the huge variety available to you.

Murphy Beds/Wall Beds

Murphy or wall beds have been around for well over 100 years. These beds pivot at one end to store inside of a cabinet that is flush against a wall. The unit must be securely fastened to your wall with anchors made specifically for the type of wall you have i.e. concrete, brick, wooden or metal studs. Normally any size of mattress, up to 11 inches, will fit inside a Murphy bed. Bear in mind that the heavier the mattress, the more strength will be needed to raise and lower if you decide not to go with an electric system. Murphy beds can be customized specifically for your needs or you may purchase a generic kit to assemble thereby saving yourself quite a bit of money. There is an incredible array of design options available depending upon the mood you are trying to set. Some sites to visit are:

www.resourcefurniture.com/beds
design.spotcoolstuff.com/cool-furniture/hideaway-murphy-bed

Murphy beds are widely available. Pages and pages of local companies and those that deliver can be found on the net by typing "murphy beds" in the Google toolbar. Prices range from under five hundred dollars for the "do-it-yourself" beds to a few thousand for the bed, assembly and installation.

ZZZ Chest™

www.fu-chest.com/zzz_movie.html

The ZZZ Chest™ is another interesting bed concept. The ZZZ Chest™ currently has three designs and five finishes ranging from country to contemporary. The price point is fairly decent at around $2000 for a double size and as it is "stand alone" there is no need to adhere it to a wall.

Zoom-Room™

This is a stand alone remote controlled Murphy bed. As with the ZZZ Chest™, there is no need to adhere it to a wall. There are standard packages as well as the option to fully customize. The Zoom-Room™ works best on non carpeted areas. As well, you must ensure all bedding is removed or safely tucked away to prevent the sheets from being tangled in the mechanism. The price point is around $5000.

www.zoom-room.com

Coffee Table and End Tables

Having a place to put your drinks while sitting on the sofa is an idea that I have found is often overlooked, but should never be. When you do not have a coffee table, it appears as though you have not thought about the needs of your tenants. A coffee table is a well used piece of furniture that *must* be installed in your property.

When choosing a coffee table, be it rectangular, round or oval, don't choose one that is too ornate. Select a coffee table that is the same height or a tad lower than your sofa seat cushions. As for length, the coffee table should be one-half to two-thirds the size of your sofa. When considering length, ensure the coffee table is 18-24 inches away from other furniture in the room.

Sometimes the sofa you have chosen comes with an ottoman. This is a wonderful option because of the versatility.

- You are able to create a coffee table with the ottoman by placing a large tray on it.
- It can be used for separate seating should more guests stay or visit in the property
- It can be pushed up against the sofa to create a single bed
- It can be used for the purpose of putting one's feet up.

I have used the matching ottoman on numerous occasions and the result is always an upscale look.

You will want a distance of about six feet from your coffee table to the media center. Scale down the coffee table width if this is not the case, but always have one.

If your room has less space than mentioned above, I have installed two small cube ottomans side by side, creating a coffee table by placing a tray on top of them to bring it all together. These cubes can be found at accessory and furniture stores and they are small but create what you need. Plus, you now have created extra seating space.

Matching your end tables to your coffee table is the easiest way to continue the creation of continuity in your room. Ensure your end tables have a distance of at least a three-inch space from your nearest wall when nestled up to the sofa and 18-24 inches from the closest other piece of furniture. If you cannot accomplish this, consider one end table or no end tables. Having one end table is fine, it will not look out of place and your tenants will appreciate the extra table. Having no end tables is not the best solution, but I wholeheartedly believe that it is better than having a crowded room. If you find that you can not fit end tables in your property, then you must get a standing lamp to place beside the couch. Good lighting is a must.

Match the wood colour of the coffee and end tables to the wood colour of your dining chairs if all these items are in one large room.

Media center

A media center with doors instead of open shelving is the best option. Over years of renting, you will find that individuals leave books and DVDs for the next tenants. Or perhaps you will want to add some books and DVDs. In any case, placing these items behind doors decreases the look of clutter dramatically. Doors also hide the wires for you electronic devices which can get fairly tangled (how I don't know, but they do) and unsightly.

As for colour, the media center can stand out on its own if that is your preference. You can go safe and match the wood of the media center to the wood of the coffee and end tables or you can go with a different colour. Whatever the colour is, I would go darker. So, if your wood is dark brown, go with either a dark brown media center or black. Any colour is fine, as long as it is darker. A lighter coloured media center will make it look like you didn't know what you were doing. A darker coloured media center or one that is glass and/or stainless steel will make it look like the media center is an attraction in itself.

Ensure the media center is not smaller than your television which will be at least 42 inches. A few inches longer on each side of the TV is important. I prefer at least 5 inches on each side making it look clean and streamlined.

If you are opting to mount your television a media center is still a must to house the DVD player and CD player and to hide unsightliness.

Should you be mounting, hiding your wires is crucial:

- You can add an electrical outlet and cable behind your television,
- You can hire an electrician to install an electrical outlet inside your wall to building code,
- You can purchase a wire cover to run the length of your wall. If you choose this option, paint it the same colour as your walls.

If you are preparing a property for executive rental, a desk and executive chair would be very much appreciated by the tenant. Ensure the desk you purchase has at least one drawer. The colour can match your existing wood tone or be that of a darker shade.

Final Words

The functionality of furniture now is amazing. I have seen coffee tables that transform into desks, end tables that transform into dining tables and desks that convert into beds. There are so many inspiring pieces of furniture. If your space is very limited, there are solutions to every problem. An excellent and fun site to visit that will amaze you is:

www.resourcefurniture.com/space-saving-video

Clei is an Italian company. The North American distributor is Resource Furniture. One thing to bear in mind is that you are paying for two pieces of furniture rolled into one. The assembler you entrust should have an array of tools and experience.

Chapter Three

Day 2 – Inventory

Appendix E, at the back of this book, is a checklist of the entire inventory you will need to create a fully equipped property. Your budget for inventory should be no more than $2500. Ensure you take Appendix E with you on your shopping trip as well as Appendix B because this is also the day you will be shopping for window treatments. For now, let's discuss, room by room, the essentials.

Kitchen

A fully equipped kitchen is a must, absolutely imperative. What you consider well stocked may not be the same as what others think of when considering this.

If you follow the recommendations below you will be covering all the bases. A vacationer or executive traveler will put up with a lot of things, but lack of kitchen inventory will probably mean never having that tenant book with you again and he or she will never recommend you to his friends or family.

If you have opted to have your property represented by a property management company, review the inventory they require in a property. Chances are you will not have to purchase

> *Take some granola with you for energy*

any additional items. A management company would not dismiss you as a client because you have too much kitchen inventory, in fact, it is the opposite. They would be impressed with the forethought.

Now, where exactly do you spend your money? Unless stated otherwise, look for bargains when purchasing the below mentioned items. For the purpose of fully equipping a property, a toaster that is $15 is just as good as a toaster that is $50. All of the items on the list should be found inexpensively except for pots, pans, knives, towels, linens and a microwave if one does not come with the property.

Toaster – 2 slots large enough for bagels is fine.

Kettle – thinking strictly of safety, ensure you get one with auto shut off.

Coffee Maker – 8 to 10 cup, again, ensure auto shut-off.

Cutlery and cutlery tray – the cutlery you purchase should be strong extremely hard to bend.

Garbage Can/Recycle Bin.

Knife Block Set – this is where you spend your money. Ensure knives are of excellent quality, like Zwilling J.A. Henckels™ or another with a great reputation. Check customer reviews on websites if you have any doubts. Without good knives, even Gordon Ramsey can't properly cook, and you'd certainly hear him swear.

Knife Sharpening Stone.

Ice Cream Scoop.

Plastic Cups (8) – for children and adults to take to the pool, beach or hot tub.

Colander – stainless steel or plastic is fine.

Cork Screw.

Pitcher – plastic is preferable.

Cookware – pots and pans that have great reputations are a must, like Lagostina™ or Cuisinart™. Here, you are spending some money. Many times, while searching for pots and finding sale items, I have used my phone to go onto the internet and obtain reviews of the set I am looking at. If the reviews are good, I buy. This is quick, easy and you know you are walking away with an excellent set. Purchase at least an 8 pot set. 1 – Large Pot/Lid, 1 Medium Pot/Lid, 1 Small Pot/Lid, 1 Large Fry Pan, 1 Small Fry Pan.

Glassware – 3 per person, a mixture of sizes. The key here is to look for glasses with minimal or no pattern. Replacement of items is much easier if they break for you want to keep with the continuity of the glasses. Mix and match glasses are really not very attractive at all.

Wine glasses – 2 per person. There is no need to purchase white wine, red wine and champagne glasses for instance. One set with no pattern so they can be easily replaced.

Blender.

Hot Pads (3) – Cork.

Coasters.

Cutting Board – purchase plastic, it is not porous like wood and will not dull your knives like glass.

Dinnerware (32 piece set, maximum 4 individuals, increase as needed) – 8 dinner plates, 8 side plates, 8 bowls and 8 coffee cups. Ensure they are plain white with no pattern. I always purchase Corel™ for a few reasons. One, Corel™ has been in business forever and broken dishes are very easily replaced. Two, you can purchase just a few plates or bowls at a time because they are sold separately as well as in a set. Three, they are hard to break. I can't stress enough the use of purchasing a no pattern, plain white set. If you don't, over the years, you will have a mismatched set and this is just not acceptable.

Fruit basket – excellent purchase for on the table or counter.

Measuring spoons and cups – these items can really range in price. I normally purchase plastic because my idea here is to just purchase the least expensive. A correct measurement is a correct measurement no matter the packaging.

Casserole Set – again, I would purchase Corel™. One deep bowl with lid and one shallow bowl.

Can opener – spend a little bit more money on the can opener. Going for the cheapest will just frustrate your tenants because some are very difficult to use.

Mixing bowl set – large, medium and small. This is good for mixing desserts, entrée ingredients, as well as useful for salads.

Roaster with lid – purchase a medium size and look for inexpensive. I usually find mine for under $10.

Grater.

Vegetable peeler.

Tea pot and sugar and cream containers.

Salt and Pepper grinders – filled – especially pepper. Pepper people love pepper.

Garlic press.

Dish towels and tea towels – 8 of each. I normally purchase this many because tenants normally like to accumulate the dirty ones before starting the washing machine. I purchase white ones as they are easily cleaned and stains can be removed without discolouring them.

Utensil set (including a spatula, pasta fork, soup ladle, slotted spoon and salad tongs) and holder – Get a stainless steel set or a dark plastic set as a light plastic may discolour over time e.g. from spaghetti sauce. If you are purchasing a holder, there is no difference between one for the counter or one for the drawer, whichever you prefer.

Barbeque utensils – brush, tongs and spatula.

Paper towel holder.

Dish rack and bottom – stainless steel or plastic is fine.

Pizza pan.

Scissors – check to see that scissors are not included in your knife block set so you are not purchasing two.

Oven mitts.

Placemats (6) – plastic, not cloth for a few reasons. One, the ends will not curl after a wash; two, they will stay looking good longer; and three, they are easy to wipe. Purchase them in earth tones.

Plastic food containers – for leftovers, in a variety of sizes, microwavable.

Knife sharpening stone.

Table Mats – one per person.

Bathroom

Multiply everything listed here by the number of bathrooms you have.

Shower Curtain and Liner – a solid earth tone colour is warm, inviting and not assaulting in any way like some vibrant shower curtains are. You are trying to create an oasis in this room as opposed to creating energy. If you prefer patterns, ensure the pattern is the same, or of the same colour family; being a shade darker or lighter than the background of the curtain.

Hooks – if you can, purchase a shower curtain and liner with built in hooks. If this is unavailable, then plastic is fine, there is no need to spend money on elaborate hooks. These will only be appreciated once, for about 5 seconds and then never be thought of again.

Towels – 2 per person of Bath, Hand and Face cloths. Opt for a better quality towel and don't purchase commercial grade. Thicker and softer is the goal as they will continue to hold up after numerous washes retaining their softness. Look for white towels with no pattern or a white pattern that is not very discernable. White towels are easy to clean and a stain remover can be used on them without changing their colour. They are also very easily replaceable.

Floor/Shower Mat – One per sink – One in front of the shower/bath – White.

Hair Dryer.
Plunger – black – one only.
Toilet brush – one only.
Soap dish/pump and optional cup.
Waste basket.

Bedroom

Multiply everything listed here by the number of bedrooms you have.

Clock radio with battery – a battery is essential in case there is a power outage.

Duvet, duvet cover and shams (two sets) – it is advisable to purchase a duvet and duvet cover over just a comforter for hygienic reasons. The comforter will more than likely be too big to wash in the available washing machine and too big for the dryer. A duvet cover is easily removed and washed ensuring it is fresh for your next tenant. Even though clean sheets will be added to the bed with each new tenant, a dirty comforter will make your attempt to be hygienic moot. Again, I like white in case the cover needs to be treated with a stain releaser. Stain releasers may dull colour making your duvet cover look very old very fast. As well, vibrancy is not wise in a bedroom, it should be a place to feel relaxed and not overstimulated. I love to use a white duvet cover and pillow cases, perhaps with a bit of a shimmery straight line pattern, because this so reminds me of upper end hotel rooms. It brings to the user a relaxing, inviting and clean feeling.

Flat sheets (2), fitted sheets (2) and pillow cases (4) – the shams mentioned above can act as pillow cases, ensure you keep this in mind when purchasing otherwise you will end up with too many cases. The sheets and pillow cases should have a high thread count. Linens with a thread count of 600 or more is a luxury that will have your tenants coming back for more. It is also an excellent item to mention on your website. Stores like Homesense™, Winners™ or Home Store™ are a great resource for linens. Save your money on items like the toaster and put it towards linens. You will notice that I prefer two of each item for each bed. Tenants may need to use another set should an accident happen in between times when the cleaners are scheduled to come. Ensure they have an alternate set. Purchase two of everything for each bed and if you opt to purchase a convertible bed, an air mattress or the like, make sure there are two sets for each one of these items as well.

Mattress protector – even though we have purchased a stain and bug resistant mattress, I still like to go the extra mile and purchase a protector.

Pillows – again, this is place to spend some money. A pack of two pillows at Wal-mart for $5 is not acceptable. These pillows will become lumpy in less than 6 months and your tenants will wish to say a few words to you about that. The best pillow money can buy is not realistic either since everything boils down to budget when preparing a vacation or executive property. A mid-range pillow is completely acceptable. The average price should be about $25 per pillow. When you are standing in front of them at the store, feel free to get do a quick internet search on your phone and read the reviews of the brand; then buy with confidence.

Pillow protectors – 2 sets per each bed.

Hangers – 20 per each bedroom closet.

Television – a flat screen of no less than 32 inches. There are many different brands of televisions. A recognizable name is a good bet, be it Panasonic™, Samsung™, Sony™ or the like.

Living room

Television and remote – a flat screen of no less than 42 inches. As mentioned above, there are so many different brands of televisions. A recognizable name with good reviews is your best bet.

DVD player/BluRay and remote.

iPod docking station and stereo – if you can get one with an am/fm radio as well that is a bonus. If not, then:

AM/FM stereo.

The DVD player, iPod docking station and stereo do not have to be the best quality items. Something mid-range with good reviews is completely acceptable.

Wireless router – if the building is not wireless, purchase a wireless router based on the square footage of your property with additional coverage for the patio, deck or yard. Many routers are easy to install, but be sure to ask the salesperson the difficulty level of the install. I have found that they know the steps involved and will guide you to one that has easy setup.

For Executives

If you have purchased a condo for corporate use there are a few items to get that would be much appreciated. Very simply, they are:

Pen/Pencil holder.

Paper or file holder.

Trash can.

Floor protector.

For Vacationers

Having a few amenities for the vacationer will go along way in ensuring a pleasant stay. The forethought put into these items is an added bonus that your tenants will greatly appreciate.

Why would someone want to come to your area? What activities does your area offer? Supply some basic necessities to make their stay more enjoyable.

For a beach vacation some ideas might be:
- Beach towels
- Beach chairs
- Sand toys
- Outdoor toys like soccer balls, footballs, badminton and tennis rackets, birdies and tennis balls
- Cooler
- Umbrella (sturdy)
- Floatation device for children – Boogie boards, noodles

For a hiking vacation:
- Backpack containing:
  - Map
  - Whistle
  - Flashlight
  - Waterproof matches
  - Rain gear
  - Water bottles

For a golf vacation you might include:
- A backpack containing:
  - Tees
  - Golf balls
  - Ball markers
  - Towel
  - Ball mark repair tool
  - Pencils

One of the best places I have found to purchase the above mentioned items is Costco™. If you don't have a membership, it is well worth getting for the cost savings will more than pay for the membership itself.

At the bottom of Appendix E, there is space provided to add the items you wish to include.

There are some items that are helpful no matter what type of vacation activities you offer, such as:

- Drying rack for swimsuits or ski equipment
- Tray for wet shoes or boots
- Large bin to harbour the items you purchased.

There are always going to be some items your tenants will need that your budget does not allow. Luckily, there are many companies that cater to the vacationer by offering items for rent.

Items such as cribs, playpens, strollers, cabanas, bikes, kayaks, paddle and surfboards, snorkel gear, tents, camping equipment, GPS receivers etc. are, more than likely, readily available in area.

Do a quick Google search by typing in "vacation equipment rental + your area."

Once you have found a company you believe would cater to your tenants, give them a quick call to introduce yourself and ask if they will give a discounted rate to those who rent from you and utilize their service. Ensure you include this information in your guest book under an easy access tab.

Miscellaneous

Below is a list of items that are needed but do not fit into the above-mentioned categories. These are essential to ensure your tenants feel at home. It is best to get a few supplies to start off your first tenant. From there, when supplies run low, other tenants will purchase these items creating a steady stream of supplies.

Dishwasher tabs and soap.

Toilet paper – two rolls per bathroom to get your tenants started.

Laundry soap and softener sheets – small sizes.

Garbage bags.

Light bulbs – extra light bulbs for all fixtures.

Hangers – if you have a front hall closet, purchase 20 hangers.

Batteries for remotes and clock radios.

Upright bagless vacuum – if you have any carpet or area rugs in your property – upright is much easier to handle and will not damage the corners or your walls as a vacuum that you drag.

Floor fans (2) – essential if you do not have air conditioning or ceiling fans.

Broom and dustpan (2) – one each for inside and outside.

Laundry basket.

Iron – ensure you purchase an auto shut-off for safety reasons.

Ironing board.

Mop and pail, and cleaners for Linoleum and Hardwood. The Swifer Sweeper works great.

Dark coloured cleaning cloths.

Cordless phone – I prefer to purchase a set of two; one for the kitchen or living room, and one for the master bedroom.

Smoke and CO_2 detectors and extra batteries.

Fire extinguisher.

Fly swatter.

First Aid Kit.

Drawer Liners.

Aluminum Foil.

Plastic Wrap.

Small Sewing Kit.

Guest Comment Book.

Owner's Closet Lock – for your own personal items, keyless or otherwise.

Keyless entry lock – by far the best way for tenants to enter and exit the rental. Extremely secure and no chance of lost keys. Purchase one with a key lock as well which you or your house cleaner will hold in case of battery failure. Batteries fail after approximately 2 years.

The best places to get the majority of the above mentioned miscellaneous inventory are places like Canadian Tire™, Superstore™, Wal-mart™ and Target™ with the exception of the keyless entry lock which should be purchased at a hardware store such as Lowes™, Rona™ or Home Depot™. There is nothing wrong with shopping around, but try to buy the majority of your items in one place, one trip, if at all possible. Going from store to store looking for the best deal wastes time, gas and actually cuts more into your pocket book that choosing only one or two stores to get inventory.

Window Treatments

If you have opted to install window treatments yourself, today is the day to purchase these items. There is really no need to go to a custom store if you are doing this yourself. Lowes™, Home Depot™ or Rona™ is fine. Once you have chosen your blinds, based on the criteria mentioned earlier, the hardware store will cut your blinds to the specific sizes. If you have opted for curtains, you can, as well, purchase those at the previously mentioned stores. Sticking with your known criteria, ensure the curtains fall to just above the floor in the living room with about one inch to spare. As for the bedroom, the curtains can fall to just below the window. Ensure the curtains and/or blinds are the same throughout the entire property. This will provide the continuity you need.

Patio Set

There is no need to spend a lot of money on this item, but there is a need to have it looking good and be comfortable. Tenants of your property will want to be outside when the weather is nice and do so in comfort. These can be found at the above mentioned stores.

I find it imperative to ensure that the patio table is large enough to hold plates and cups for your guest comfortably. On beautiful weather days your tenants are going to want to spend time outside and that includes dining outside. Use the same measurement specifications for the dining room table to determine the size of the patio table if you opt for a circular table.

Test out the chairs to see if they are comfortable. There really is no need to purchase chairs with cushions on them. I have found many comfortable chairs that do not have cushions. Cushions become wet and tenants will be hanging these to dry sometimes more often than actually sitting on them.

My recommendation is to get plastic chairs that look like wicker. Stay away from wicker and iron as wicker looks very bad only after one year, graying and splintering, and iron rusts. As well, we are avoiding cushions so iron would be so uncomfortable. Once cushions are wet, they stay wet for a long period of time. Sitting on iron is not conducive to relaxing.

Supply Kit

Today is also the day to get your supply kit. These supplies are located at the hardware store where you will be to get your blinds/curtains. You will find a "tear out" list of needed supplies in Appendix F at the back of this book. The supply kit is very thorough. I have accounted for possibly any situation you can come across. This is the kit I take with me to every job, minus just a few items I don't think you'll need. You may find that you do not wish to purchase all that I mention, and this, of course is your prerogative, but nothing is more frustrating than not having something available to you and wasting valuable time and energy going to the store. It's up to you, but I find it better to be safe than sorry.

Supply Kit Inventory

- Carrying bag
- Hammer
- Dish soap
- Nails, screws and hooks (variety pack)
- Felts for under furniture (if you have hardwood)
- Glass cleaner
- Scissors
- Paper Towel Roll
- Wire – for pictures
- Wire cutter (if you think scissors will work you're wrong – been there, done that)
- Screwdriver with a variety of heads
- Adhesive remover like Goo Gone™ or Goof Off™
- Exacto knife
- Touch up stain in brown and black
- EZ clips for use if installing blinds and or curtains

P.S. Bring your laptop if you have purchased Wi-Fi and a DVD movie to check that the DVD player is working properly.

Drop off your inventory at the property and call it a day. You did well today!

Chapter Four

Day 3 – Furniture and Inventory Placement

Today is a bit of a waiting and being patient game. Your delivery drivers and assemblers have been scheduled to arrive today, and you are going to be placing the inventory you purchased yesterday.

If you are planning to install curtains/blinds yourself or need to install the smoke and CO_2 detectors, now is the time. This is the perfect opportunity as it will keep you busy while waiting for the delivery drivers and assemblers.

The first thing you will want to do is remove all of your bedding and towels from the carrying bags and place them in the washer for their first cleaning. Turn the cycle signal to "on" so you hear when the cycle is complete to immediately put them in the dryer.

After the window treatments have been installed it is time to tackle the kitchen and bathroom inventory. Begin with opening larger boxes, like your pot and pan box. As you take out the items, replace the protective cardboard and foam immediately back in the box. I cannot stress this enough, for the amount of clean up you will have to do in the end will be reduced dramatically. Work your way down to smaller boxed items, removing items and placing the smaller boxes in the larger boxes. You will usually be able to fit about four smaller boxes in one large box saving considerable space and ensuring you will not create a tripping hazard as they start to accumulate.

Clean all pots, pans, plates, bowls, glasses etc. to ensure

there is no dust and your first tenants have clean items to eat off of and prepare their meals in.

One thing that saves tremendous time is checking which items have a price tag on them and placing a wet paper towel over the tags. They will be on some items such as plates, soap dish and tumbler. Let this sit as you then go on to placing other items. In about 10 minutes come back and the price tag will be easily removed. There may be some extra adhesive left over. Use the adhesive remover in this case.

Keep all of your instructions for the small appliances you have purchased and place those in a cupboard not normally used, such as the one above the fridge keeping your easy to reach cupboards available for inventory. Extra inventory items such as additional light bulbs and batteries should be placed here as well.

Ensure you have one cupboard that remains empty. This empty cupboard may then be used for dry goods.

Placement for best results:

When placing your items in cupboards, ensure placement makes sense to the tenants. Tenants will first search the most likely place where items will be. It is very frustrating to have to scour drawers and cupboards for an item that is in the wrong place. Chances of these items being placed again in the spot you have originally chosen will, as well, not happen. Make it make

---

Designate an "owner's closet" (ensure it is not the kitchen pantry) that will house items for your own personal use when you yourself vacation at the property. Install an entry lock.

---

sense and tenants will keep it as such.

Kitchen

The wooden knife block set, fruit basket and paper towel holder should go on the counter.

Glassware and dinnerware should be placed above the sink and close to the dishwasher. Salt/pepper shakers, the sugar/cream containers and the tea pot should be placed in this cupboard as well.

Casserole set and mixing bowl set should be placed in a bottom cupboard with the toaster, kettle, coffee pot and blender. Place the colander and the grater in this area as well.

The next bottom cupboard should house the entire pot and pan set.

Place the roaster, pizza pan and cake/lasagna pan in the bottom drawer of the oven if you have one available, if not,

---

> ***Cut and line cupboards and drawers, line oven with aluminum foil.***

---

then just the next available cupboard.

Cutlery should be placed in a top drawer close to the dishwasher and sink, but if the dishwasher and sink are far apart then place the cutlery closer to the dishwasher. Cooking utensils should go in the next drawer down unless you have purchased a standing holder for them, then they should be placed by the stove.

The next drawer down from the cutlery should also house the scissors, measuring spoons, cutting board, can opener and cork screw. If cutting board is too large, slide it in with the pots and pans.

A third drawer should house the dish and tea towels as well as oven mitts, table mats and hot pads.

Continue placing your inventory until the delivery drivers arrive. As they begin to unload, directing them where to place the furniture is very important as they will not wish to keep repositioning. Give them your attention. If your delivery drivers are your assemblers as well, great, if not, then the assemblers should have arrived by now as well. Once the furniture has been placed you will be able to resume your placing of the inventory.

If you were able to acquire from them removal of packing items, kindly ask if they could also remove the boxes and bags of your inventory. Asking kindly often works and will save you some valuable time later on. Sometimes giving them a bit of money for doing this will make them much happier to do it for you.

As your furniture is getting assembled, continue on with placing your inventory. Guide the assemblers to do one room at a time, beginning with the bedroom(s) ensuring they *fully complete* one room before moving on to another room. Ensure the assemblers place the bed and nightstands a few inches away from the wall so you can plug in the alarm clock and lights without having to push these items out of the way later.

After the bedrooms are done, have them move on to the living room/dining room. In the living room, ensure they assemble the media center first and then the desk, coffee and ends tables, dining table, chairs, bar stools and finally the patio set. Chances are you have not purchased your patio set with the furniture store, but have gotten it at another location, if this is the case work a deal with the furniture store assemblers for a little "extra" money to assemble these items for you.

In order of priority:
1. *Bedrooms first – Bed before anything else.*
2. *Living room/dining room second – Media center, desk, coffee and end tables, dining table, dining room chairs,*

bar stools.
3. *Outdoor third – patio table and chairs.*

Bathroom

Place the tumbler and the soap dish.

Remove the freshly laundered towels from the dryer and put two towels on the racks. Drape a hand towel over these and then a face cloth to finish it up.

Fold the remaining towels and place them under the sink or in an appropriate cupboard if you have one. Place the hair dryer in this same area.

Place the wastebasket beside the bathroom cupboard.

If you have a longer countertop, I often like to place a hand towel folded in three in this area or a basket filled with hand towels and spa-like items. It takes up space and adds a nice decorative flare. Adding accessories by the bathtub also helps to make the room feel like an oasis.

Hang the shower curtain and liner so that the liner is inside the tub and the shower curtain is on the other side. Push these items off to the side showing the faucet.

Place the plunger and toilet brush in a utility closet if one

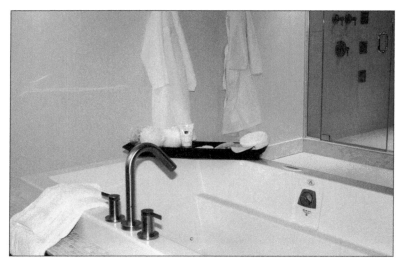

is available to you. This same place should house the ironing board, iron, and all other items such as the pail, cloths and vacuum. If you do not have such a closet, hopefully these items will fit beside the washer and dryer. You will always find a place that is non descript.

Place the extra linens on a shelf in the master bedroom as well as the beach towels if you needed to purchase these items. While here, hang the hangers in the closet.

As soon as the assemblers finish with one room, ask them to lift the ends of the furniture so you can place the felt pads you previously purchased to protect your floors.

Put on the mattress pad and pillow protectors. Remove the bedding from the dryer and make the bed. I love creating a hotel-like atmosphere with the bedding, making hotel corners and a tight fit. Your house cleaners more than likely will know how to do this, if not show him/her how you would like the bed made in the future on Day 5. There is a reason hotels prepare their beds this way; nothing feels more luxurious and clean than a well made hotel-like bed.

If the sheets appear to be wrinkled, give them a quick once over with the iron you have purchased. At times I will find that only a few wrinkles have appeared and I often plug in the iron close to the bed and take these wrinkles out with the bed already having been made. It's quick and easy. This may seem a little over the top, but touching up here and there creates the look you are trying to achieve before taking pictures.

If you are not sure of how to make a hotel-like bed, here are a few tips:

1. After the fitted sheet has been placed, place the flat sheet so that you can fold it over at the top of the bed once with a fold width of about 10 inches. Smooth the sheet.

2.   Tuck in the sides of the flat sheet under the mattress. Hold the corner of the sheet at the bottom of the bed with one hand and pull it against the tucked side sheet. This will make a diagonal fold.

3.   Fold your duvet in thirds and place at the foot of the bed. Lay your pillows and the bed will now be ready for decoration the next day.

Plug in and place the alarm clock on one nightstand. Ensure it is set to the correct time and on a variety of stations.

Mount or place the television on the dresser, chest or appropriate item you purchased for this reason. Plug in and test to ensure all channels are being received.

Outdoor Items

Place your outdoor items, beach chairs, toys in their appropriate place. My suggestion is to place these items outside. I once stayed in a vacation rental where all the beach toys were placed in a closet in the master bedroom. The bedroom had carpeting and removing the items from the shelving resulted in sand and small shells being dropped on the carpeted floor. The shelves were lined with sand. This is not hygienic in an interior space so avoid this at all costs; even if you have a bedroom floor with no carpet.

Moving from one room to the next should be very seamless. The items you need to work with should be ready and waiting for you if you have managed your assemblers well.

Living room

Once your bedrooms are done, start in the living room with the assembled media center. The assemblers should be working on the coffee, end tables and desk (if you have purchased one for your executive needs).

Unless you wish to incorporate a hard core workout in your schedule today, ensure all furniture is placed in the designated spots you have assigned them. Moving furniture once the assemblers have gone is a chore I avoid doing myself, as nothing will make you more tired more quickly and strain your muscles.

Beginning with the media center, place and plug in the television ensuring all channels are being received. Place and plug in the DVD, iPod docking station, stereo and Wi-Fi. Check to ensure these are in working order.

If you have purchased a desk for the purposes of renting an executive suite, place the pencil holder etc. on the desk.

Rearrange chairs and shift table if you find you should, and place bar stools.

Have your assemblers move on to the patio and assemble the table and/or chairs if they have agreed to do so.

Finally, look around at what you have accomplished.

Good day today!

Everything has been unpacked and placed. All packing materials have been removed.

Do a quick clean up. Vacuum, dust and sweep. Ensure all debris is out of the property.

Tomorrow we will be shopping for art and accessories. Relax tonight and see you tomorrow!

Chapter Five

Day 4 – Art and Accessory Purchase and Placement

To appeal to the majority of your tenants, we have previously incorporated earth tones. Now we are going to bring in vibrancy through art and accessories.

Your main goal is to get your individual tastes out of the equation and only use decorative pieces that attract the majority of the extended stay tenants.

Whether one is on vacation or in an executive suite, the goal is to feel comfortable and relaxed in what feels like home. For a vacationer and an executive this is one of the ultimate goals.

There are fundamental rules to decorating and we are going to be touching on these as we look for and purchase art and accessories. It's going to be really simple. So, let's get started.

Art

Sizing

The size of your art is so very important. It has to be in scale with the wall it is adhered to and to what is placed beside and underneath it. The eye loves to go down "in steps" and up "in steps" that is why the decorating rule of thumb of 1/2, 2/3, and 3/4 is so important and should not be ignored.

When placing either one singular piece or a series of pieces placed together, the art should take up 2/3 to 3/4 of the area or space you are trying to cover. It is imperative if placing a series of pieces together that the space between each piece is equal and

> ## *You will need two cars or a van.*

your groupings make up an odd number.

The art you choose should be colourful otherwise your rental may look too washed out and diluted. Look for art that makes you feel energetic. Stay away from pastels as these colours seem to date themselves very easily.

If you are purchasing art for a vacation property look in local stores catering to tourists and outdoor markets and you will find amazing handmade authentic pieces in your price range. Here is where geographical location comes into play. There is no need to go to an art gallery. The look we are going to create will feel rich without having to spend a lot of money.

If you are decorating an executive suite, I would stay mostly with mainstream art that you would find at Winners™ or HomeSense™. Choose abstract (non life-like) pictures because they can be incorporated into a contemporary interior easily. Abstract art has no rules so you will be able to find and match with ease.

Choose a store that carries a large selection of decorative accessories besides art (vases, bowls, pillows, rugs etc.) so that you are not traveling from store to store looking for items. This is overly time consuming, not to mention frustrating.

Once you have found a piece of art that you like, choose a colour in that art to expand upon. The colour you choose will come through in the additional decorations your purchase.

The psychology of colour is useful knowledge to have when deciding which colour you wish to expand upon. As you will see below, different colours evoke different moods in people.

Warm Hues	Cool Hues
Warm colours create a mood of excitement & warmth, stimulating activity and creativity.	Cool colours have passive, calming qualities that aid concentration and can create a mood of peacefulness and tranquility, reducing tension.
Red Energy, Passion, Power, Excitement	**Green** Health, Regeneration, Contentment, Harmony
Orange Happiness, Confidence, Creativity, Adventurousness	**Blue** Honesty, Integrity, Trustworthiness
Yellow Wisdom, Playfulness, Satisfaction, Optimism	**Violet** Regalness, Mysticity, Beauty, Inspiration
Neutrals Neutrals are great for adding stability and balance in a room. They include white, black, gray and colours that contain any significant amount of gray.	

(www.para.com/colour-101/psychology-of-colour)

Once you find one piece of art that you believe would work in the property, and you find the colour in that art that you would like to expand upon, continue to find other pieces of art that have this specific colour in them. This will be fairly easy to do if you are looking at a large selection.

If you feel you are second guessing; stop. Nothing is more damaging to the creative process than questioning yourself.

> ***Scale your art to furniture that is placed underneath it. Use the rule of 2/3 to 3/4.***

If by chance you are not finding additional art that goes with your chosen colour, don't panic, the idea here is to be versatile and compromising. Relax and it will all come together. Look at your art again and choose a different colour to expand upon. Please keep in mind that, first and foremost, we are creating continuity.

If "going with your gut" makes you feel uncomfortable, take the Benjamin Moore™ Timeless Neutrals brochure with you to the store. Match the complimentary colours shown beside your main wall colour with the art. Super easy, and flawless.

Purchasing:

Living room

- one large piece above the sofa or two to three matching small pieces set horizontally and even;

- one piece on an opposite wall next or above another piece of furniture or point of interest like the fireplace, singular chair or plant for instance

Dining room

- one large piece, or a series, set on wall closest to the dining table.

Bedroom

- two pieces of art, each above the nightstands approximately 3 inches higher than the lamps. This may seem very high should your headboard not be high enough. If so, then place the art to the left or right of the lamps approximately two inches away from the lamp with the bottom of the picture being in the middle of the lamp.

-or-

- A larger piece or one to two pieces above the headboard. I often do not do this because I have a deep irrational fear of art falling on someone's head while they are sleeping. This has never happened to

me, therefore the irrational thought, but it still gives me the sweats.

If you have an obvious place where a picture should go, consider placing art here as well. The room will seem too bare if you don't address this perfect place for art.

Bathroom
- One piece per bathroom is usually sufficient

When choosing art for your bathroom remember that what we are creating is a spa- like experience. Your art therefore should not be very colourful and vibrant. In fact, it should be just the opposite. The art should have nature's colours in earth tones staying in the white, cream or taupe hues possibly combined with green and/or brown foliage. These combinations of colours

are incredibly serene and relaxing, creating the environment you wish to express.

It is not absolutely necessary to place art in the bathrooms. If there is an obvious space where art should go I do place it, but sometimes these areas have towel racks on them. If this is the case, no picture is fine. We are going to be placing towels and bathroom accessories in a decorative fashion and this will make up for the fact that there is no art if this is the case.

Blankets/Throws and Pillows

Now that you have found your art and the colour that you wish to expand upon, find one throw blanket for each bedroom and one for the living room. It may be good idea to take the art that you have chosen directly to the blankets. If you go by memory, you may choose a colour that is just "off" of what you actually have, having a different undertone. If this happens, it will create disharmony.

Once you have your blankets, take these to the decorative pillow section. Ensure the pillow coverings can be removed for washing for hygienic reasons. Hold the pillows up to the blanket you have chosen. Choose two to four pillows for the living room. The pillows do not have to be all identical; just ensure that the colours in the blanket are displayed in the pillows.

Do this same process with the pillows you choose for the bedrooms. One to two pillows per bed will suffice. There is no

need to purchase more than this, but if you wish, no more than three or four.

Lighting

Purchase a table lamp to be placed on the every end table and the nightstand.   Proportion is very important and using a lamp base that is 1/2 and a lamp shade that is 2/3 the size of your table base will work well.   This doesn't have to be perfect measurement; being close, like horseshoes, counts.

The colour of the lamp base can be one of three things:
1. The base can be in the same colour tone as your walls.

-or-

2. You can choose a metallic, black, or glass base. These different elements will add some flare to your property and add a nice decorative element,

-or-

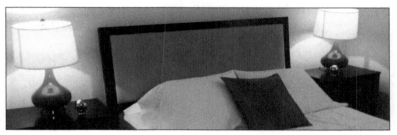

3. Choose a lamp base that is the same as your accent colour if it is not blindingly vibrant.

The shades of your lamps should, again, complement your wall colour, not necessarily your accent colour. Light, medium or dark beige colours will work well.

You can also have fun with the lamps and shades if you are decorating a vacation property. Choosing a lamp and shade that complements your location is fun and enhances the vacation experience. For example, a twisted iron base that looks like a tree branch in a colour that is naturally found in our environment is amazing in a place like Whistler for instance. A lamp made of shells would look great in Hawaii.

If you find that your living room is a bit dark, purchase

a standing lamp. Standing lamps are also perfect for ambient lighting.

Accessories

Moving on to the accessories; we are looking for items that can be grouped in fives, threes or just ones. Accessories that either have your chosen main colour in them or the absence of colour altogether. Either one will be perfect. Again, don't over think.

If you are choosing an accessory with colour in it, it can be a solid colour or the colour can be minimally shown; as long as it is there. If you wish to display the absence of colour, choose something with a lot of texture like etched glass or silver hues; something that catches your eye and the light. You can also mix the absence of colour with your chosen colour. For example, a glass etched bowl filled with decorative balls of your chosen colour. This way, the colour comes in but is not overpowering.

The accessories should be minimal. Less is more. You do not want your tenants to feel that they are in a cluttered room and accomplishing this with accessories is very easy. Clutter

is associated with uncleanliness. A few beautiful pieces placed here and there is much more appealing.

Living Room

What you choose to place on your coffee table will depend

entirely on its size.

Rectangular: a rectangular table has a lot more options for decorative pieces than any other type of coffee table. Normally, I like to do one of two things; place one piece dead center of the table or put four pieces, one larger piece by itself on one side of the coffee table and a grouping of three on the other side.

These items can be a bowl or platter for the larger item and three tall thin vases, books or candles in varying heights and widths for the grouping. I personally like the idea of a bowl for the coffee table because this allows a place for the remote controls and magazines.

The coffee table is also a good place for the coasters you have previously purchased. Keep your coasters where your tenants can see them, otherwise, out of sight out of mind.

If you are looking for more of a minimal look, another option is to place a grouping of three items across the table about two to three inches apart from each other. One thing that is very

> *Artificial plants require much less maintenance. Good quality plants look extremely real. Don't expect your tenants to water live plants.*

appealing is to place three identical artificial small plants in this manner. Ensure your plants are identical in everyway including the vases. This is very clean looking and Zen-like.

Circular: with a circular table place one decorative piece in the center of the table, be it a platter, or a larger vase. Leave the remainder of the table open and uncluttered for placing items such as drinking glasses.

Ottoman; two small ottomans pushed together; or small tables: place

a tray on the ottoman(s) creating a coffee table by having a solid, flat area to place drinking glasses. The tray can also display a few local magazines and/or remotes.

End Tables: place the lamps on your coffee table and you already have one piece of "art", but I like to add a bit more as the end table will seem bare without one more piece. The accessories you use on the end tables do not have to be the same on both

sides, though I have done this and it is very balancing. One end table may also display your coasters if you choose not to put them on the coffee table.

Media Centre: leave the media center as is and do not add accessories. Items have already been placed here and adding more may appear cluttered.

Desk: if you have chosen to install a desk in your property.

Placing accessories here is preferable. I would stick with typical accessories for an office such as a small artificial plant or book ends.

Dining Room

Dining room table: There are many items to choose from, a larger

vase, a platter, a grouping of three or five in varying heights, or, to bring the outdoors in, a small artificial plant. If choosing a plant, ensure it looks as real as possible. Also ensure that the housecleaner knows to dust any plants on a regular basis.

Dining room credenza: Use the same guide for a rectangular coffee table.

Bedrooms

Night Stands: moving on into the bedroom, I like to match the accessories on the bedroom nightstands. The bedroom is usually

a smaller room and matching accessories really makes the room feel balanced. To create a warm and relaxing feeling consider placing a 5x7 picture frame on each nightstand of a nature shot (flowers, horizons etc.).

If you are not placing the television on the dresser then place three identical items across this area. This creates a Zen

like feeling and your tenants will find this very soothing and relaxing.

Whatever you choose for your accessories, always remember to place in odds.

Appendix G for art and accessories at the back of this book is to be used a bit differently than the previous appendices. You are going to be using this once you are in the store and not

before. It will help guide you as to what you have and what you need. When you have so many items to purchase, and so many rooms to purchase for, a guide will help tremendously. Your mind will be focusing on so many things that forgetting items will happen naturally.

As you decide on items, write what you have purchased in the area of the room where the item is to be placed. This will give you a clear understanding of what you have, what you are missing and what you still have to purchase.

Filling in empty spaces

More than likely you will find that there are spaces in your property that are empty and seem to be missing something. Artificial plants, vases with sticks or standing lamps are great options for these areas.

Think functionality when placing items in your property. If

you find you have space beside the entrance door, a table placed here is very functional. Another option is to place a bench in this area. The forethought that tenants may wish to sit down to put on their shoes will be much appreciated.

If you have placed your media center on a long wall, flanking it with two plants or vases filled with tall sticks such as bamboo

is gorgeous. This will fill in the area without taking up space.
Do you have a corner in your room with nothing in it? A plant
here would be beautiful, as would a sculpture or a decorative
chair.

If you have a gas fireplace an artful piece placed to the side
is beautiful.

Mirrors placed in the property are also a nice added touch.

They can be placed conveniently by an outside door or in an empty space. Mirrors add a different dimension. They make a room look larger and brighter. If you are opting to place a large standing mirror ensure that you attach it to the wall.

Area rugs

Area rugs add a feeling of warmth to any space if you have wood, tile or any other hard surface flooring. They also add a nice decorative touch by tying in the other accessories. To keep the feeling of relaxing harmony in the room ensure the rug you choose is one of warm tones. This rug can have your accent colour in it, but make sure the accent colour does not entirely encompass it. This will be too stimulating for the living room.

Choosing the right size rug is very important. The items you will place over the area rug should be 3/4 the size of your rug; be it the sofa, coffee table or dining table.

If you choose to place an area rug in the bedroom(s) you can

> ### *You may wish to purchase non slip mats underneath the rugs. Mark in Appendix H if this is the case.*

do one of two things. Choose two narrow rugs or runners on each side of the bed. Ensure the scale of the rug is 1/2 to 2/3 the size of the bed. You can also purchase a very large area rug that the bed will sit upon. Ensure the bed is 3/4 the size of the area rug.

Bringing it all home

Once you have purchased all of your decorative items and have brought them to your property, the fun really begins.

Unpacking your items carefully, place wet paper towels over all price tags to let soak for about 10 minutes for easy removal. Nothing wastes time like trying to scrape off price tags. This will save you a tremendous amount of time as you will have many to remove. Follow up with adhesive remover and perhaps some glass cleaner to remove streaks.

While the price tags are soaking, remove the tags from the throw pillows and throw blankets you have purchased and place them.

Living room

Place your throw pillows and your throw blanket on the sofa, you will find that placing these items adds instant warmth to your property and completes the look you are trying to achieve. It will also add to the photos you will be taking for your website. Layering decorative elements adds depth and warmth.

Lay your area rug. If the ends are curled, they should fall on their own over the next 24 hours. If you find that after that time the corners are still sticking up, wet them a bit with some water and place a heavy object on top of the area that is sticking up. Within a short time the rug should be laying down.

Center the sofa to the rug placing it in front of or just underneath the sofa.

Set, plug in and test your lamps. The lamps can be placed in the center of your table or off to the side.

If plugging in a lamp results in a cord that could now be a tripping hazard, invest in a safe power cord enabling you now to have extra length to move against a wall and out of the way. Should this be the case, this will be one of the items you purchase the next day. Write it down in Appendix H to keep note.

Your price tags should now be able to slide off the product you have purchased easily. Place your accessories following the rule of odds; one, three or five groupings.

Lastly, it's time to hang your art. Attach a wire to the back of the picture if one is needed. Art placement is very important and this can make or break a room. Most individuals I find hang their pictures too high. Here are a few rules of thumb when it comes to hanging pictures:

- The middle of your picture should be placed at 52" from the bottom of the floor.
- If you are hanging a picture above your sofa or a chair the space between the bottom of the picture and the top of sofa should be 6"-9".
- If you are hanging your picture above a bench or table, use the rule of 52" from the floor.

Dining room

Place the centerpiece or pieces you have chosen for this area. Stand back to check the scale. If the scale seems too small it is time for a little ingenuity. Take your placemats from their designated place in the kitchen and place those underneath your centerpiece(s). Play around with them until the scale is perfect.

Hang your art ensuring that if a chair is pulled out from the table it will not touch the art.

If your dining room was large enough to hold a bar or credenza, place a grouping of varying heights in this area.

Place your area rug, if you opted to purchase one, so that the table is centered perfectly inside of it.

Bedroom

Place, plug in and test your lamps. The bedroom lamps, in this case, should be centered on your nightstand or just off about 2 inches. Place the accessory you have chosen for this area.

Hang your artwork so that it is 6 to 9 inches from the top

of the headboard. If it is a series of pictures ensure they are spaced 2 to 3 inches apart. If you opt to place a picture above each nightstand, create a group of three with the lamp and the accessory.

If the television is mounted and you have purchased a dresser or chest, place one accessory in the center, or the series of accessories in a straight line ensuring same spacing. Basically, follow the rules of decorating a rectangular coffee table.

If you have purchased one decorative pillow, place it in front of and between your bed pillows. If you have purchased two, place them directly in front of your bed pillows. If you have purchased more than two, continue to layer them so they scale down.

Place the matching throw blanket on your bed either horizontally or angled on your duvet. Either position looks amazing and very professional.

Bathroom

If the bathroom can harbour art, use the same measurement rules as with all of the other art you have previously hung.

Depending on the size of your countertop you may have

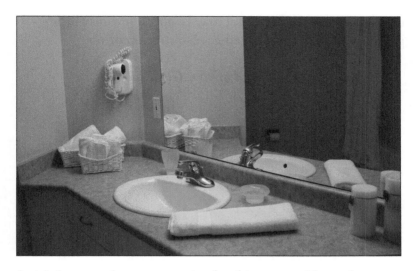

decided to purchase accessories for this room. If so, place your accessories in their appropriate groupings. By now, you have already placed your towels and laid your bathroom mat(s). All of these items combined will look well put together, filling in your countertop without taking up a tremendous amount of space.

Once everything has been placed take a look around. It may seem perfect to you or you may feel there are a few things missing; perhaps there is a misplaced item. When I am at this point, I critique everything, really paying attention to how I feel. Do I feel harmony, or is something off? Fiddling around with accessories is something every decorator does. Moving different pieces to different areas, or even moving them a few inches to the left or right can dramatically change the look and feel of the room. Play around with these, paying attention to the way you feel more than anything. When I feel aligned I know I have accomplished what I wanted to accomplish. I am sure, by following the instructions in this book, that you yourself will have this feeling.

If you find that there are few missing items, mark them

down in Appendix H. There may be just a few more things to get to make it all come together. Do this tomorrow.

I'm proud of you. Good Job!

Chapter Six

Day 5 – Finishing Up

Good morning. You have now arrived at Day 5. You are almost done. Today is an easy day. It is a small task and a finishing up day.

Start the morning out by dropping by your property and walking around it with a fresh mind, energy and enthusiasm. Do you notice anything missing? Is there an empty space that could use something? If there is, add what you need to Appendix H, get these items immediately and place them so you are at the property when the meetings you have scheduled for this day show up.

Photography

Today is the day your house cleaner and possibly the property manager are coming. While you are waiting you have the time to take pictures. Taking pictures is good for a few reasons;

- Insurance purposes, an insurance company would very much appreciate pictures to go along with the receipts you have gathered;
- Tax purposes, your accountant and your governing tax agency may need to see evidence of your business expenses;
- For your housecleaner to use as a reference of how you would like items placed and beds made until he/she is use to your place;
- For your website.

> ## *Take pictures of serial numbers for insurance purposes.*

I believe the more pictures the better. A little bit of artistic flare when taking pictures creates a professionalism you don't often see on vacation and executive rental websites. The photos are going to be taken in such a way that people visiting your site feel as if they are actually in the room they are viewing, ensuring a much more personal and intimate feel.

Hiring a professional photographer is a wise investment. You are selling your property over the internet; you wish to impress future tenants and you want your property reflected at its best. Spending money on a professional photographer is well worth it as it will definitely increase interest in your property.

Search for a photographer using the terms:

"architectural photography + your area"

Ensure they take virtual tours as well as photographs. Inquire to make sure the virtual tours are compatible with the Apple and Android market.

There is a fairly wide discrepancy in the rates of professional photographers. You should spend no more than $600 to $800 on these services. PanaViz (**www.panaviz1.com**) for example service the Hawaiian Islands and have packages starting from $500 that include virtual tours. They have set quite a high bar; don't expect anything less from the photographer you choose. Christopher Bowden is an international architectural photographer who is offering services for the cost of travel for a limited time only if your vacation property is outside of the U.S. You can inquire about him here:

www.christopherbowdenphotography.com

If you find that a professional photographer is just not in your price range, consider hiring an architectural photography student in their last year from your local college or university.

The cost will be reduced dramatically and they will use the wealth of knowledge they have accumulated in class and in the field. Enthusiasm is often high and results are often very good. The student has his/her first paying "gig" that they can add to their portfolio and benefit him or her in innumerous ways.

If you opt to take your own pictures, then the following tactics should help you tremendously. Any good quality digital camera will work for these purposes. An excellent photo editor is Adobe Photoshop Lightroom 4.

Lightroom addresses challenging light conditions and allows you to adjust shadows and highlights to create exactly what your eye saw when the photo was taken. It is highly recommended at $150.

You may even wish to try taking photos with the camera in your phone. Phone cameras have come along way from when they were first introduced. They are about as user friendly as you can get. Shooting, editing and downloading are a breeze. Apps like photowizard-photoeditor and photo fx are seemingly easy to use and both have great reviews.

The first bit of advice is to take many pictures so that you have a wide variety of choices. The extra time it takes to take these photos outweighs having to return at a later date and retake because there are not enough pictures to choose from. With a large collection of photographs you will also be able to replace photos at your whim updating your website.

Lighting

You are going to be taking series of pictures:
- Lights on, window treatments open,
- Lights on, window treatments closed,
- Lights off, window treatments open,
- Lights off, window treatments closed.

Unless you have an excellent eye for how light will fall on your furniture and fixtures, take all of these photos. You may find that one angle looks great with less light and another angle looks wonderful with more light.

I am not a professional photographer and it is difficult for me to imagine what the photo will look like as opposed to what I see through a camera lens. So, again, I ensure I have as many options as possible.

Technique

When taking pictures of a specific room, start from one corner and come in close. Take your first picture in the corner of the room, then bend your legs coming down to a half squat and take the exact same picture, move in closer, completely squat and take the last picture. The closer you move in, the lower your squat should be. Below are two photos taken from the same angle. We have only come closer and lowered our line of vision.

Once you have completed this round of picture taking,

complete the same procedure from the other three corners of your room.

If you have one long area that holds both your living room and your dining room, create your own "imaginary" corners for each area. By doing this, you will have some pictures that you wish to delete right away, but you will also have some amazing pictures.

The bathrooms, of course, are an exception to this. This process is difficult in small, tight rooms, so you may find you can only get a few pictures in. This is fine, just make sure you take the pictures from as many angles as your bathroom allows and you will find one or two amazing ones as a result.

Go above and beyond and take pictures that are rarely taken. I have seen this a few times on sites and am always impressed with the extra effort it takes to take and post more pictures. To me, this verifies that the owners of the vacation or executive rentals are proud of their property and wish to show it in its best light. You can always tell when someone just snapped a picture to put it on the site and when someone took some time to show the property. Your future tenants will be impressed and

feel more comfortable renting your property when a few extra pictures are taken and posted, as well, you will also stand out above the crowd:

- Open your cupboard doors and take pictures of your newly acquired inventory.
- Open your drawers and display your cutlery and utensil drawer.
- Photograph the extras you have added to your inventory, such as your bin or beach toys.

Don't forget to take photographs of your patio set and your view from the windows of your property.

Showing off your property in all of its glory ensures your future tenants feel extremely comfortable and assured when booking with you.

Once the photos are ready to be added to your site, consider

Hawaiian deck and interior www.vrbo.com/223523

adding text of special features to each photo such as "Livingroom with a view of the mountains" or "Granite countertops with rain showerhead". The photos will seem more personal and more authentic.

Adding a date to your photographs will put potential tenants at ease that what they see is actually what they will get. Consider adding to the text your direct contact information. This allows for instant communication. Future tenants will always scan photographs to narrow down their choices after they have chosen a location. As they scan your impressive photos a direct contact link will have them clicking or phoning more impulsively.

Housecleaner

You wish to have your housekeeper as knowledgeable about your property as possible so there are no disappointments later on. Your housekeeper will appreciate knowing exactly what to do and you will be rest assured that your property will continue to look great long after you leave.

A housecleaner with experience in vacation and executive

rentals is the best option. There are many things to do that are above and beyond a normal house cleaner's regular duties that someone with previous experience in this area is recommended.

When searching for a house cleaner ensure you check references or ask a neighbour who is also renting their property who they employ. You will need someone who is consistent, flexible and thorough. Alternatively you can check the Vacation Rental Housekeeping Professionals at

www.vrhp.org

Type in your city, province or state to see members of the association in your area.

At the back of this book, you will find Appendix I which is a cleaning checklist to give to your housecleaners to ensure they don't forget certain important items.

Of all of the things that are listed on the sheet it is imperative that the housecleaner:

- Check pillow protectors and mattress pads for stains and remove or replace.
- Check for bedbugs. In major hotels, cleaners are trained to check for bedbugs. If they see evidence that room is infected they discreetly close it off until the bugs are eliminated. If the cleaners you choose do this on a regular basis you should not have an infestation that could paralyze your rental business. Tell your cleaners to check:
  o dark spots left on bedding,
  o seams, creases, tufts and fold of the mattress.

Give strict instructions to notify you should any evidence of this.

Ensure you add the house cleaners contact information to your in-suite information binder as they may wish to have the property cleaned more often than your scheduled times. Ask the house cleaner how much notice he or she needs if tenants ask for this and include that in the information binder.

Appendix I is fairly extensive covering the changing of light bulbs to cleaning the remote control devices to checking inventory.

Maintenance Person

If you are living far away from your vacation or executive rental or if you wish a professional to handle maintenance issues, a maintenance person or company will oversee your property on a continual basis. I find speaking with other vacation or executive property holders as to who they use is often your best option.

There may be instances in which missing or broken inventory may have to be replaced. If the housekeeper you hired is opposed to the extra work involved ask the maintenance person you have enlisted to do this on your behalf. The fee you decide on should be in an hourly form of between 17 to 22 dollars per hour plus expenses should there be certain things that require some extra attention.

Concierge Service

Concierge companies who service rental properties are often all encompassing. They organize cleaning, maintenance and at times, property management as well as catering to the needs of your tenants with services such as entertainment planning, meal preparation and personal shopping just to name a few.

Checking references is so extremely important for you are now relying on another person besides yourself to satisfy the needs of your tenants. The actions of a concierge company can make or break a vacation experience. A professional organization, one that is extremely accommodating, is a must in this case.

Type in your search engine:

"concierge" or "concierge association" + your area

for a list of available companies. Ask for references and follow up.

Alternatively, if you are opting to hire a property management company to address the issue of housekeeping and maintenance inquire as to their standards. Ensure they are above or at par with what has been recommended.

The information in Appendix I is extremely important and should not be overlooked. Completing the checklist will ensure you can rest assured that your guests' expectations are fulfilled to the best of your ability. The Appendix also protects you against complaints that are false in nature because will have a record at your disposal should you need it.

The Appendix should be filled out with each departure and then faxed or emailed to you with comments and appropriate follow up prior to your guests arriving. As for the keyless entry, ensure you use a systematic approach to changing the code for the new guests such as up in fives or tens.

Alternatively, feel free to recreate Appendix I using Google Docs. Google Docs is a free service up to 5 GB and allows you to create, share, edit and download documents to your computer. I love the idea that you can also collaborate and edit in real time.

support.google.com/docs

With Google Docs you will have an electronic record as opposed to a paper record.

With the advent of FlipKey and Yelp reviews, these inspections are an absolute necessity. Maintaining an excellent reputation is of the utmost importance.

Chapter Seven

Going Above and Beyond: Working with the Statistics

Demographics

What are the demographics of the people that will be interested in a vacation or executive rental? Well, they are a lot like you:

- one third of them earn a yearly income of at least $100,000
- over 60% of them are college educated
- 90% take at least two leisure trips per year
- 75% are online more than one hour per day, and
- 90% would rent a vacation rental again and recommend them to family and friends.

(©2009 PhoCusWright Inc. All Rights Reserved.
PhoCusWright's Vacation Rental Marketplace: Poised for Change).

These individuals are in varying stages of their life. From young couples to families to empty nesters. Even though they come from varying backgrounds one thing remains constant and that is why they buy (or rent in our case).

They buy for three reasons:

- to satisfy a basic need,
- to solve problems,
- to make themselves feel good.

(http://sbinfocanada.about.com/cs/marketing/a/targetmarket.htm).

So, what are the basic needs? How do you solve their problems and make them feel good? A lot of the answers to these questions have already been presented in this book. By following my recommendations you have already positioned yourself above and beyond. What more can you do?

Let's explore further to answer this question so you are able to take advantage of history and trends; use this invaluable information to create what your tenants want and need and provide your findings on your website and in your guest information book.

Psychographics

Have you heard of Psychographics Marketing?

If not, it is marketing that answers the questions of the lifestyle, behavior and attitude of the person in question to build up a more detailed picture of who they are.

Psychographics marketing can work alongside demographic marketing to allow advertisers to promote their products effectively, in order to sell their products in the long term. Psychographics marketing leaves advertisers one-step ahead of their competition.

(http://dippykitty.hubpages.com/hub/Psychographics-marketing)

Vacationers

Psychographically speaking, there are four different types of vacationers, they are:

- **Tour Groupies**. These vacationers enjoy the convenience and ease of guided tours and prefer packaged deals to independent travel.
- **Kickin' Back Vacationers** use their vacation time to rest and relax; the effort involved in taking a foreign trip, sightseeing or even going on a cruise is not for them. They

prefer to travel by themselves or in small groups.

- **Active Adventurers** choose vacation destinations that give them plenty to do. Frequent and independent travelers, they like theme parks and sightseeing, physical exercise and outdoor recreation—especially while on vacation.
- **Ever the Spring Breakers** still go for the fun, not the sights. They like guided or package tours for the convenience.

(www.gfkmri.com/PDF/GfKMRIPsychographicSourcebook.pdf)

To Do:
- Decide what kind of tenants you wish to attract.
- Insert tabs in your guest binder for the ones you choose, name the tabs with interesting descriptions like the ones above.
- Add your researched information:
  - For **Tour Groupies** list an abundance of tours that are available with contact information, reviews and brochures.
  - Find companies that offer tours individually or use a company that books multiple tours, call and ask if they will give a discount if your tenants use their services.
  - For **Kickin' Back Vacationers** list popular beaches, if your area offers these, popular picnic sites, nice places to stroll and explain the relaxing benefits they would expect to find.
  - List yoga, mediation classes, bookstores, nearby theatres and live shows along with contact information and map directions.
  - On your website, speak of long, leisurely meals on the deck or patio, relaxing by the pool or going in the hot tub. Mention that their schedule is their own and explain that once they arrive they will have everything at their fingertips.
  - For **Active Adventures** follow the steps for Tour

Groupies
- List an abundance of activities that are available with contact information, reviews and brochures i.e. ziplining, parasailing, best mountain runs for skiing for example.
- Find companies that offer these adventures and call to ask if they will give a discount if your tenants use their services.
- **Ever the Spring Breakers** will be interested in guided tours as well as more night life activities.
- Research hot night spots and restaurants in your area and include those in your information binder. Mention those with happy hour.
- Add places that are often frequented by Hollywood's elite if there are such places.
- Write of the best shopping, discount stores etc.

You can also use this information to distract certain tenants from your property. Should you decide that Ever the Spring Breakers are not the type of tenants you want simply do not add this information and emphasize things like quiet nights on your site.

Corporate Executives

By reviewing the psychographics of the traveling executive provided by the Corporate Housing Providers Association we can discover intelligent ways to impress and keep tenants as well as have them return and recommend your property.

Though 85 percent of business travelers state that traveling is a key reason why they like their current job, their priorities are very different. Business travelers can be categorized into six key psychographic groups:
- Experience – Hungry
- Hyper Connected

- Cost Conscious
- Home Focused
- Seasoned, and
- Green.

Experience–Hungry travelers make up 39 percent of those surveyed. These people try to balance business travel with personal interests, scheduling in as much free time as possible so they can explore new destinations. In their briefcase, the experience-hungry traveler is most likely to carry a camera, a city map and, most importantly, a shopping list. This group illustrates that corporate travel now often incorporates personal priorities as well as business.

To Do:
- Supply maps in your guest information book of your geographical area. As these individuals are pressed for time, ensure you print directions from your property to points of interest from a source such as MapQuest. Shopping malls and tourist sites should not be neglected.

The **Hyper Connected** group comprises 23 percent of corporate travelers. This group is most often married and although they don't necessarily enjoy traveling for work, they like the opportunity to develop business networks. This group takes many different wireless devices with them and they are very focused on their business objectives.

To Do:
- Your guest book should include recommended restaurants and a description of the ambiance each one provides. Business lunches and suppers will be high on the hyper connected list of things to do.
- Networking activities may include events such as golf. Ensure you include directions to and from highly rated courses and possibly some complimentary passes.
- Ensure you have installed wireless internet.

- Ensure the designated work space has file and pen holders. Add pens and note paper for something a little extra that will be much appreciated.

The **Cost Conscious** traveler makes up 14 percent of travelers. They are most likely to work for a company with less than 50 employees and they make sure that value for money is the key priority in every business trip. By following the directions in the book to this point, you have already given and demonstrated the great value your property has over others on the market. Really take advantage of their key priority and

- Include discount coupons to restaurants, fun activities, car rentals, groceries and the like.

Seven percent of travelers make up the **Home Focused** group. They enjoy traveling the least and are between 36 and 45 years old. People with young children find themselves in this group.

To Do:

- If your corporate tenant is staying for a fairly long length of time, ensure you have all the linens, towels, pillows etc. for the extra beds that are in the property. Often family will come and visit for the weekend.
- Again, wireless connection is so important so the family can Skype with ease.

Seasoned travelers (six percent) are the most frequent travelers, making around 25 business trips a year. For these people, travel is a core part of their work routine and half of them have assistants to help them organize trips.

To Do:

- Attract these tenants by providing them with the services of a local concierge in the area. Ask the concierge service if they will offer a discounted rate and/ or any complimentary services. Services may include unpacking upon arrival, packing upon departure and grocery shopping to name a few.

Finally, the smallest, yet potentially the fastest growing group is the **Green traveler**. At just four percent of those surveyed, this group only travel by plane if there is no other option and have frequently considered investing in projects to reduce CO_2 emissions to offset their travel.

To Do:

- Proudly display on your site anything you have, or your cleaners do that are "green" in nature. Do you have recycle bins in the area? Are the cleaning agents you use environmentally friendly?

As this is the fastest growing segment of business travelers, any implemented "green" alternatives should be listed. The site should be continually updated with any additional advancement you have made in this arena.

©2008 Expedia, Inc. All rights reserved. CST# 2029030-40, 2083922-50. SOURCE: Egencia http://press.expediainc.com/index.php?s=43&item=241

More Exciting Statistics! (vacationers and executives)

Fifty per cent of people interested in vacation rentals said children had a significant effect on their decision of vacation destination. (*TripAdvisor Second Annual Vacation Rentals Survey*). Sway tenants with children to stay with you by creating a tab with information about activities that appeal to children 5-14 years of age and, of course, include this on your website.

Thirty-nine per cent of vacation travelers are concerned that the property will be as advertised (*TripAdvisor Third Annual Vacation Rentals Survey, 2011*).

- The advent of TripAdvisor, FlipKey and Yelp reviews have made inspections imperative (see Appendix I).

Ensure you don't miss this very important step.

- Virtual tours and still photography are a must. Remember to date these on your site every six months or so to show current condition.
- Aside from new pictures or decorative elements, update your photos and virtual tour immediately should there be any significant changes to your property.

Of those travelers staying in a vacation rental for the holidays, thirty-six per cent say they'll cook a special holiday meal.

- Ensure you have above average pots, pans, knives and cooking utensils.
- Discuss the brand names of these on your site. Mention Henckel™ knives if you have them.

(HomeAway® Vacation Rental Marketplace Report 2011)

When asked what travelers liked the most about vacation rentals as a lodging option:

- 28 percent cited more space (ensure you follow spacing rules in Chapter 2!)
- Mention square footage and even possible room size on your site.
- Add a layout of your property to your website.
- Compare the square footage of the average hotel room in your area with your property. See **www.miamirentme. cz/gallery/hotel_aparman.jpg** for an example. Incorporate a similar idea.
- Couple this with quoting hotel room rates. 13 percent of people like that rentals were often less expensive than hotels. In fact, go one step further and work out the price to stay in your property for one week compared with the price to stay in a nearby hotel for one week.
  Item costs such as:
- Hotel room rate vs. your rate.

- Cost of typical meal eating out vs. cost of groceries eating in.
- Include cost of parking, tips and laundry service with hotels.

The cost comparison will be astounding.

Twenty-three per cent of travelers enjoyed having access to a full kitchen.

- Keep well stocked and check inventory on a set and continual basis.

Twenty-nine percent of travelers either always or often stay in the same rental year after year. Of the travelers who stayed in a vacation rental in the past:

- Twenty-two percent booked their rental home more than six months prior to the trip.
- Thirty-four percent of travelers booked their rentals between three and six months out.
- Twenty-two percent booked between one and three months out.
- Just two percent of travelers booked their vacation rental less than one month out.
- Update your site to include price discounts for late bookers

If you wish to take advantage of the 2% of travelers that book less than one month out, by all means do so, but another option is to contact **www.geronimo.com**.

Geronimo will rent your vacation home on your behalf while helping your favorite charity. Their website is worth a look. You can also see more information about them at the back of this book.

Thirty-six per cent of travelers who have rented in the past have stayed in a vacation rental for a milestone life event, such as a wedding, birthday or reunion.

- Have a party planning section in your information book as to where to go to get balloons, streamers, customized t-shirts etc.
- Have information on shopping malls and outdoor markets for gifts.

When deciding between different rental properties, the key influences cited by respondents are:

- Photos of the home (42 per cent); so you can:

  Post pictures, lots of them, date them and continually update the date.

  Post virtual tours.
- Traveler reviews (27 per cent); so you can:

  Ask your tenants to please review on FlipKey, TripAdvisor and Yelp.

Most travelers find out about vacation rental properties on vacation rental property websites (70 per cent).

There is an abundance of rental property websites. Do a Google search and you will see pages and pages. Which one do you choose? To get you started, here are a few to look at

- **www.vrbo.com**
- **www.geronimo.com**
- **www.homeaway.com** in the US, **.ca** in Canada and
- **www.vacationrentals.com**

The Top Fives

Campaya's Rental Property Market Trends for 2011 is worth a look. This extensive report covers what tenants value and search for when inquiring about rentals. It is worth noting in your website if your property has any of the below to offer.

Top 5 Holiday Rental Location Requirements:
1. Airport
2. Supermarket

3. Beach
4. Children Activities
5. Restaurants

To 5 Holiday Rental Activities
1. Golf
2. Cycling
3. Fishing
4. Walking
5. Skiing

Top 5 Must Have's
1. Internet
2. Satellite Cable/TV
3. Swimming Pool
4. Quality Bedding
5. Comfort

Top 5 Appliances
1. Air Conditioning
2. Washing Machine
3. Heating
4. Dishwasher
5. BBQ

Creating a great looking rental is sound judgment. Adding the understanding of why and how your target market will use your rental and communicating that effectively ensures you have a winner.

Lastly, 94% of renters want the most value they can get from a rental. Show them yours.

Chapter Eight

Final Words

If there is anything I can say to end this how-to book it would be to trust in the process. I have taken all my knowledge, all my learning over the years, and have discovered the most streamlined approach to fully furnish and equip properties.

Many suggestions in this book are basic and straight forward, expanding on known statistics and following some of the most utilized rules of decorating. I know I have mentioned this many times before in this book, but it really does boil down to "how you feel." Pay attention to that and you will do fine.

P.S. Send me pictures of what you have done. I would love to see them!

Thanks, Anita.

Bonus Chapter

Guest Information Binder

The guest information binder is your chance to get personal with your tenants. Unlike hotel binders which focus mainly on the amenities of the hotel, a vacation or executive rental binder informs tenant of not only your property (significantly reducing the number of calls you receive for information), but of a vast majority of activities available to them that they might not otherwise be aware of. This helps to create a wonderfully memorable experience.

Make two copies in case one goes missing from your property or post online.

You will need:
- 3 ring binder with a front cover clear plastic insert
- Clear sheet protectors
- Tab dividers

Create the binder information first and then purchase the above mentioned materials so you know exactly how many protectors and dividers to purchase.

To be inserted in front of binder:

- Name of Property
- Full Address and telephone number
- Contact information of yourself (if you opt to give this out), house cleaner, maintenance person, concierge

Welcome first page, with history of the home or property.
Tabs (refer to Psychographics):

- Important Contacts
  - Police
  - Fire
  - Ambulance
  - Private security
  - Directions from property to local hospital emergency, walk in clinics, dentists
- General Information
  - ATMs, currency exchange, courier stations, post office, airport, train and bus stations, business centers, places of worship
- Contract
  - Check in instructions
  - Check out instructions
    - Where to leave keys/parking pass etc. upon departure
    - Any specific instructions such as to remove kitchen garbage, strip sheets off bed etc.
- Property
  - Who has access to the home and when
    - Exterminators, gardeners, garbage pick up schedule etc.
    - Pool/hot tub instructions
    - Tennis lights, outdoor lights
    - Barbeque instructions
    - Heating/air conditioning/heated floor instructions

- Internet access, resetting instructions
- Location of all major and minor equipment and appliance instructions including TV and DVD, batteries, light bulbs
- Property layout and location on map, aerial or otherwise
- Copy of condo association rules if applicable
  - Smoking areas, barbeque areas, pool/hot tub/weight room hours and rules
  - Complex layout, aerial map
  - Location of garbage and recycle bins
  - Visitor parking location (if not on complex layout)
  - How to allow someone entry if in a secured door building
- Vehicle (if providing)
  - Where registration, insurance and manual are located
  - Where first aid, tool kit, candles, blankets etc. are located
  - Any special instructions such as type of fuel
- Activities
  - All manner of physical activities with maps from the property and brochures
    - Golfing, beaches, hiking, night life
  - Coupons
- Shopping
  - Directions from property to malls, fairs, kiosks, grocery stores, liquor stores, markets
  - Party planning stores (streamers, balloons, grab bags), flower stores, personalized cakes (how much notice they need), cupcakes, custom t-shirts, etc.

- Dining
  - Recommended restaurants for breakfast, lunch and dinner and map from property. Personalize with recommended dishes
  - Take out and delivery restaurants – ethnic variety
  - Provide menus
  - Coupons
- Services (if no concierge)
  - Recommend specific spas, tour guides, personal trainers, yoga instructors, alternative healers (Reiki, acupuncture), dermatologists, make up artists, hair stylists, spiritual advisors, chauffeurs, chefs, and caterers
  - Brochures, coupons, discounts
- Living Like a Local
  - Directions from property to little known non tourist sites
    - Hiking, shopping, night life, parks, picnic sites etc.
    - Personalize with your own experiences, eg: "the hiking trail highlighted on the map is our favourite with the most variety of plant life", "dancing at this venue doesn't get going until midnight".
  - Directions from property to these non tourist sites
  - Local customs, streets to avoid during the night
- Other amenities
  - Rental businesses
    - Sports equipment, baby equipment etc.
- For Kids
  - Directions from your property to the kid friendly activities such as playgrounds, parks and zoos
  - Provide discount coupons

Gift Baskets

Providing a gift basket upon the arrival of your guests is a thoughtful and very much appreciated thing to do. Often guests do not wish to go shopping as soon as they arrive. They are often tired and wish to relax. A gift basket filled with items they may need upon arrival will often result in smiling faces.

Your house cleaner or concierge service can do this on your behalf. The price should be per basket in this case and not based on an hourly fee. Ensure all contents remain constant so buying in bulk allows you to save more money.

There is no need to get too extravagant with the items; they should not be pricey. It is the thought that counts. Include items such as local coffee, tea, wine, nuts and chocolate for example. You may also include basic toiletry items such as small soap, shampoo and conditioner. The toiletry items can be purchased in bulk by companies who supply hotel chains such as:

www.gilchristsoames.com

They are one of many who have an excellent reputation. Type "hotel" and "soap" to see a variety of other companies.

Some local companies will give away samples, cups, stickers, notepads etc. as advertising in the hope that your guests will visit their establishment during their stay. Inquire with these establishments, often they are pleased to help.

What to Put Aside

FF&E or "Furniture, Fixtures & Equipment" represent all moveable objects that are placed within the property. The more highly rated your property, the more likely you're FF&E will be more costly and higher end.

It is imperative that you put aside a reserve fund to cover the cost of the inevitable replacement of the FF&E. To monitor the replacement cost of certain items follow these guidelines:

Replacement
Within the first 5 years – Paint and mattresses.

5-10 years – Media (televisions, iPod docking station etc.), carpets, curtains, fitness equipment.

10-15 years – appliances, furniture, decorations and lighting.

All kitchen and bathroom inventory will be on an "as needed" basis.

15-20 years – general renovating – updating of tiles, countertops, faucets etc., pool, hot tub.

There are a few schools of thought on the amount of the reserve fund, generally speaking:

- 1% of gross monthly rental in the first year, 2% in the second, and so on, all the way up to 5% in year five; or
- 3.5% of gross monthly rental starting with your first month.

A word to the wise, as your reserve fund accumulates you may be tempted to upgrade or replace before the need actually arises. Do not. This will only deplete your reserve fund and you may find yourself in a situation where you will not have enough funds for necessary items.

The above mentioned timeline and reserve fund amount are for properties that are not in need of extensive renovations already. You will notice that they pertain more to a condo complex than an actual single family dwelling. Please adjust your reserve fund accordingly to account for older model condos or single family dwellings.

About the Author

Anita Ericksen lives in Edmonton, Alberta and has been actively consulting, furnishing and equipping executive and vacation properties since 2006. She has one husband, one son and two cats. This is her first book.

You can visit her at **www.anitaericksen.com**.

VACATION HOME OWNERS:
Promote Your Vacation Rental to Supporters of over a MILLION Charities!

Increase your Rental Income. You select the available dates and you set the rates and we promote your spare weeks. You keep half the rent and half goes to charity. You're in full control of where the charitable piece goes! Geronimo even gives you a one click way to promote your property on Craigslist!

Help a Charitable Cause. Donate half the rent (or donate all of you're feeling especially generous) to your favorite cause or let the renter choose the charity.

Much Better than Silent Auctions! If you've ever helped out a silent auction by donating a spare week, you'll love Geronimo. com!

FREE to List Your Property
www.geronimo.com

Geronimo!
vacation rentals for charity

Appendix A

Inspection

Item	OK	Not OK	Comments/Follow-up
Kitchen:			
Cabinets/Countertop – securely fastened, proper alignment, squeaks			
Ceiling – water spots or stains			
Sink – scratches, leaks, caulking			
Backsplash – grout, cracks, stains			
Handles – securely fastened, general shape			
Stove, Fridge, Microwave – good working order, stains, rust			
Faucet – general appearance, water flow, leaks. drainage			
LR, DR, Bedrooms, Hallways:			
Walls/Trim – cracks, water damage, dents, scratches, popping nails			
Closets – proper alignment, squeaks, dents, scratches			
Stairs – squeaks, loose handrails			
Door – well fitted, squeaks			
Bathrooms:			
Cabinets/Countertop – securely fastened, proper alignment, squeaks			
Ceiling – water spots or stains			
Sink/Bathtub/Shower – scratches, leaks, caulking, drainage, water pressure, stains, mold			

Backsplash – grout, cracks, stains			
Handles – securely fastened, general shape			
Door – well fitted, squeaks			
Walls/Trim – cracks, water damage, dents, scratches, popping nails			
Toilet – leaks, securely fastened, water pressure			
Exhaust Fan – working properly			
Miscellaneous:			
Washer/Dryer – water leakage or mold around the supply hoses; dryer exhaust, unclogged, vents, good working order, stains, rust			
All Doors – well fitted, squeaks			
Windows – well fitted, insulated, cracks, broken glass, proper alignment, open/close with ease			
Floor/Tile – cracks, grout, stains, seal			
Floor/Lino/Hardwood – dents, scratches, water damage, varnish (hardwood)			
Floor/Carpet – stains, buckling, lifting, water damage			

Appendix B

Window Measurements:

Address:
Suite:

Blinds - inside of a window – depth, height and width. Starting with the width, you will measure from inside the trim at the top, middle and bottom before moving to the height, which you will measure inside the trim at the left, centre and right.

Drapes - outside trim to outside trim - height and width. Also measure the wall space surrounding the trim.

Drawings:

Appendix C

Room Measurements

Address:
Suite:

Draw an outline of your room including all recesses, windows, doorways or jut-outs.

Example:

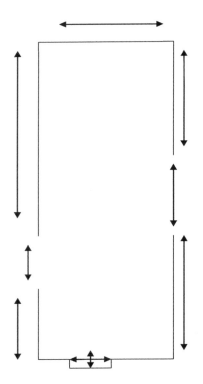

Drawings:

Appendix D

Furniture Inventory Checklist

Living Room	√
Sofa/Sectional/Sofa bed	
Love Seat/Chair/Chaise	
Entertainment Stand	
Coffee table (Ottomans)	
End table(s)	
Master Bedroom	
King/Queen Bed	
Night tables (2)	
Chest/Armoire/Bookshelf	
Mattress/Box Spring	
2nd Bedroom	
King/Queen Bed/Sofa bed	
Night Table	
Dresser	
Mattress/Box Spring	

Dining Room	
Table & Chairs	
Counter/Bar Height Stools	
Credenza	
Office/Work station	
Desk	
Chair	
Floor Mat	
Balcony/Patio/Deck	
Chairs	
Table	
BBQ + utensils + cover	

Notes:

Appendix E

Equipping Checklist

Kitchen	
Microwave	
Blender	
Garlic press	
Knife block set	
Toaster – slice/bagel	
Kettle – auto shut off	
Glassware – tall/short – 3 per person	
Barbeque utensils	
Wine glasses – 2 per person	
Dinnerware	
Casserole set	
Roaster with lid	
Plastic cups - 2 per person	
Knife sharpening stone	
Coasters	
Placemats	
Colander	
Ice cream scoop	
Vegetable peeler – rubber tip	
Cork screw	
Can opener	
Grater	
Sugar/Cream containers	
Tea pot	
Cookware (10-12pce)	
Pitcher	
Plastic food storage containers	
Spatula, Pasta fork, Soup ladle, Slotted spoon, Salad tongs	
Utensil holder	
Dish rack and bottom	

Pizza pan	
Salt & pepper containers - filled	
Dish towels (8)	
Tea towels (8)	
Oven mitts	
Scissors	
Paper towel holder	
Mixing bowl set	
Coasters	
Measuring spoons/cups	
Fruit basket	
Cutting board -plastic	
Hot pads (3) – cork	
Coffee maker -auto off	
Cutlery + Cutlery tray	
Garbage/Recycle can/bags	
Table mats	
General	
Drying rack	
Large bin	
Tray for wet shoes or boots	
Bathroom	
Shower curtain /Curtain liner	
Hooks	
Bath towels – 2 per person - white	
Hand towels – 2 per person - white	
Facecloths – 2 per person - white	
Bathmat – one per sink/bath/shower	
Soap dish/Pump	
Cup	
Waste basket + bags	
Toilet brush	

Plunger – black	
Hair dryer	
Bedroom	
Duvet cover (2)	
Duvet	
Flat sheet (2)	
Fitted sheet (2)	
Pillow cases (4)	
Mattress protector	
Pillows (2)	
Hangers (20)	
Pillow protectors	
Television	
Clock radio with battery	
Living Room	
DVD player/Blu Ray	
IPod docking station	
AM/FM stereo	
Wireless router	
Television	
Miscellaneous/Supplies	
Fire extinguisher	
Floor fans	
Broom & pan - 2	
Laundry hamper/basket	
Fly swatter	
First aid kit	
Iron (auto shut-off))	
Ironing board	
Mop/Pail /Cleaners	
Dark colored cleaning cloths	
Smoke/CO2 detectors	

Batteries	
Upright vacuum	
Toilet paper	
Drawer liners	
Laundry soap/Softener	
Dishwasher tabs/Soap	
Cordless phone	
Light bulbs – all fixtures	
Owner's closet lock	
Keyless entry lock	
Aluminum foil/plastic wrap	
Drawer liners	
Small sewing kit	
Hangers for front hall closet (20)	
Guest comment book	
Office/Work station	
Paper/file holder	
Floor protector	
Pen/pencil holder	
Trash can	
Beach Vacation	
Beach towels – one per adult person	
Beach chairs – one per adult person	
Sand toys	
Outdoor toys	
Cooler	
Youth floatation device – boogie board/noodle	
Umbrella - sturdy	
Hiking Vacation	
Backpack	
Hiking map	
Whistle	

Water bottles (2)	
Waterproof matches	
Flashlight	
Golf Vacation	
Backpack	
Tees	
Pencils	
Golf balls	
Ball markers	
Small towel	
Ball mark repair tool	

Notes:

Appendix F

Supply Kit Checklist

Carrying Bag	
Hammer	
Dish Soap	
Nail, screws and hooks	
Felts	
Glass Cleaner	
Scissors	
Paper Towel	
Wire (pictures)	
Wire cutter	
Touch up stain	
Exacto knife	
Multi head screwdriver	
Adhesive remover	

Notes:

Appendix G

Art & Accessories

Living Room	#
Master Bedroom	
Other Bedroom (s)	
Dining Room	#
Bathroom	
Other Bathroom(s)	
Office/Work station	

Balcony/Patio/Deck	

Notes:

Appendix H

Other Notes

Appendix I

House Cleaner Instructions, Inspections and Audit

In addition to your regular deep clean please ensure the following is done as well.

Item	OK	Not OK	Comments / Follow up
Living Room:			
Check for rips or stains on furniture Clean under cushions and furniture			
Ensure legs are sturdy.			
Ensure TV, DVD, radio and iPod docking station are in working order			
Clean remotes, check batteries			
Check phone for dial tone			
Clean information binder and comment book (check if full)			
Bedroom(s):			
Dresser/Chest/Nightstand – empty and wipe down all drawers			
Empty all closets			
Check for bedbugs			
Ensure linens are free of stains and that there are two sets for each bed			

Check that alarm clock is set to the correct time			
Bathroom(s):			
Check curtain liner/shower door for mold			
Check all bath, hand, face and beach towels for stains and holes			
Ensure toilet flushes properly			
Ensure exhaust fan is working properly			
Check for dripping faucets			
Dining Room:			
Ensure legs are sturdy			
Check furniture for water marks			
Kitchen:			
Check for leaking faucets			
Empty dishwasher and ensure it is working			
Clean oven, ensure it is working and time is correct			
Clean all cupboards/ drawers/fridge. Take food to predetermined location.			
Clean salt and pepper shakers			

Fill ice cube trays with fresh water and place in freezer			
Ensure all inventory is in its proper place			
Miscellaneous:			
Check all light bulbs and replace if needed			
Ensure thermostat/air conditioning is working and set to 69 degrees			
Ensure fire and CO_2 detectors are working			
Dust, clean window coverings			
Ensure all windows are cleaned and locked			
Clean patio/deck furniture and wipe down toys; clean patio floor			
Clean and check backpacks			
Clean bin			
Check iron is free of deposits and water			
Check first aid kit			
Empty vacuum canister			
Change key code			
Place all keys, fobs etc. on kitchen counter			
Clean washer, remove lint from dryer			

Additional Instructions:			

Please check to ensure the inventory on the attached sheet is in the rental. If something is missing notify me immediately.

(Attach a list of all inventory in your property).

Index

Accessories
    Art...18,24,67-80.
    Blankets/throws...77,99.
    Lamps...73,78-9,86,93,99.
    Pillows....77,99.
Accessory, placement
    Bathroom...76.
    Bed...73.
    Coffee table
    Desk...87.
    Dining room credenza...89.
    Dining room table...88.
    End tables...81.
    Media center...87.
    Night stand...89.
    Sofa...36.
Active Adventures...117.
Activities, top fives...124.
Additional sleeping...33.
    Murphy bed...34.
    Sofa bed...33.
    Trundle bed...33.
    Wall bed...34.
    Zoom-Room...35.
    Zzz Chest...35.
Adobe Photoshop Lightroom...107.
Air mattress...34.
Antimicrobial protection...27.
Appliances, top fives...125.
Art
    Bathroom...76.
    Bedroom...73.
    Dining room...72.
    Executive purposes...68.
    Hanging...99.
    Living room...70.
    Scaling...67.
    Size...67.
    Vacation purposes...68.
As advertised, statistics...121.
Attract tenants...25,67,117,120.
Barstools...29.
Bathroom...45,5976,101.

Accessories...101.
Art...76.
Inventory...19,45,59.
Set up...14.
Bathroom, refurbish...9,13,134.
Bed bugs...24,27,112.
Bedroom. See also furniture
Accessories...73.
Art...73.
Bed...25.
Chest...25.
Dresser...25.
Inventory...46.
Mattress...26.
Nightstand...25.
Platform bed...26.
Set up...58.
Benjamin Moore...11,70.
Blankets...77,101.
Booking, statistics...115.
Budget...41, 50.
Campaya...124.
Chair/chaise...32.
Ceiling light...13,28.
Circular dining table...27.
Chest...64,100.
Children, statistics...121.
Christopher Bowden Photography...108.
Cleaning...17,113,158.
Closet organizer...25.
Coffee Table...35-37.
Colour consultant...11.
Concierge service...113.
Corporate Housing Providers Association...118.
Cost comparison vs hotel...122.
Credenza...91, 102.
Damaged items...23,25,33,140.
Decorating...69,81,103.
Delivery drivers...23,57.
Demographics...117.
Desk...60,89.
Dry cleaning...34.
Earth tone...70.
Empty spaces, filling in...95.
Equipment rental...52.

Events, statistics...121.
Ever the Spring Breakers...119.
Executive art...70.
Executive chair...40.
Executive inventory...50.
Extra seating...38.
Fabric...29.
Flooring...16,100.
Foam mattress...36.
Furniture
        Assemblers...23.
        Damaged items...23.
        Insurance...24,107.
        Shopping...29,49,54,70.
        Stain removal...18,23,29.
        Style...24,26.
        Type...26.
Furniture assemblers...23.
Furniture spacing...57.
Futon...36.
General inventory...43.
Geronimo.com...125.
Gift baskets...135.
Gilchrist Soames...135.
Golfing inventory...51.
Google Docs...116.
Green travel...123.
Guest information book...131.
Handyman...115
Hiking inventory...51.
Home Away...126.
Home Focused...121.
House cleaner...65,90,107,113.
How to take pictures......110.
Hyper Connected...121.
Inspection...124,140,160.
Items to rent...52.
Key influencers, statistics...126.
Keyless entry...53,116.
Kickin' Back Vacationers...118.
Kitchen, statistics...125.
Kitchen inventory...21,43,59.
Kitchen refurbish...134.
Lamps...39,80.
Laptop...56.

Leather...31-33.
Lighting
        Ceiling...12.
        Lamp, standing...81.
        Lamp, table...80.
        Track...30.
Lighting, photography...109.
Living room
        Art/Accessories...72,101.
        Concept...31.
        Inventory...49.
        Set up...31,60,67.
Maintenance person...115.
Making beds...65.
Management company...44,115.
Mattress...28,35,48,66,114,136.
Media Center...28,39,60,67,89.
Miscellaneous inventory...52.
Missing items...95,107.
Murphy bed...34.
Must Haves, top five...125.
Nano Stain Terminator...29.
Neutral tone...70.
Night stand...27,91,102.
Odds (placing items)...94,101.
Office chair...40.
Ottoman...38,86.
Owners' closet...53,58.
PanaViz Photography...108.
Para Paints...71.
Patio furniture...60,67.
Philosophy...8.
PhoCusWright...117.
Photo FX...109.
Photography
        Insurance...107.
        Lighting...109.
        Reference...107.
        Serial numbers...108.
        Taxes...107.
        Technique...110.
Photography student...108.
Photowizard – Photoeditor...109.
Pictures...107.
Pillows...49,79,101,102.

Placing accessories...79,86,91-96,101.
Placing decorations...90-95.
Placing inventory...57-68.
Portrait of American TravelersSM...9.
Positioning
        Bed...27.
        Chair/chaise...34.
        Dining table...29.
        Sofa...32.
        Television...31-32.
Pot lights...14.
Professional photographer...107.
Property management company...44,115.
Protecting mattress...29,65,114.
Psychographics...118.
Psychology of colour...70.
Pull out bed...33.
Rate, statistics...124.
Rectangular, coffee table...35.
Reinforcing bed...33.
Repeat tenants...7-9,23.
Reserve fund...135.
Resource Furniture...36,40.
Retain tenants...7-9,23.
Requirements, top fives...126.
Room measurements...18,26,31,55,144.
Round, coffee table...35.
Savings...28,31,35.
Sbinfocanada...117.
Scaling, art...67.
Setting up
        Bathroom...47,61.
        Bedroom...48,60.
        Executives...50.
        General...52
        Golfing...51.
        Hiking...51.
        Kitchen...43,59.
        Living room...49,67.
        Miscellaneous...52.
        Outdoor items...52,54,66.
        Vacationers...50.
Serial numbers, photography108.
Shelving unit...27-8.
Shrinking ...34.

Sizing, art...67.
Sofa...32,38,101.
Sofa bed...35.
Space, statistics...124.
Stain removal...23,32,34,46,48,114.
Standing lamp...81.
Statistics...117.
Supply kit...55.
Table lamp...80.
Taking pictures...107.
Taxes, photography...107.
Technique, photography...110.
Television...28,40,49,66.
Throws...77,101.
Top Fives...126.
Tour Groupies...118.
Track lights...30.
Trip Advisor...126.
Trip Advisor Second Annual Vacation Rental Survey...123.
Trundle bed...33.
Vacation art...68.
Vacation equipment rental...52.
Vacation Rental Housekeeping Professionals...114.
Vacationer inventory...50.
Vacationrentals.com...126.
Value, statistics...118.
Vrbo.com...112,126.
Wall bed...34.
Wall colours...12,70,80-1.
Website...27,49,107,119.
Website, statistics...126.
Window treatments...54.
Wood...25,39.
Working kit...56.
YPartnership/Harrison Group...9.
Zoom-Room...35.
Zzz chest...35.

CPSIA information can be obtained at www.ICGtesting.com
Printed in the USA
LVOW01s1546090713

342088LV00012B/19/P

9 781894 953979